Writing for Conferences

Writing for Conferences

A HANDBOOK FOR GRADUATE STUDENTS AND FACULTY

Leo Mallette and Clare Berger

GREENWOOD

AN IMPRINT OF ABC-CLIO, LLC
Santa Barbara, California • Denver, Colorado • Oxford, England

Library of Congress Cataloging-in-Publication Data

Mallette, Leo.

Writing for conferences : a handbook for graduate students and faculty / Leo Mallette and Clare Berger.

p. cm.

Includes bibliographical references and index.

ISBN 978-0-313-39406-5 (hard copy : alk. paper) — ISBN 978-0-313-39407-2 (ebook)   1. English language—Rhetoric—Study and teaching (Higher)   2. Critical thinking—Study and teaching (Higher)   3. College readers.   4. Academic writing—Study and teaching (Higher)   I. Berger, Clare.   II. Title.

PE1408.M3375   2011

808'.042—dc22   2011002273

ISBN: 978-0-313-39406-5
EISBN: 978-0-313-39407-2

15   14   13   12   11   1   2   3   4   5

This book is also available on the World Wide Web as an eBook.
Visit www.abc-clio.com for details.

Greenwood
An Imprint of ABC-CLIO, LLC

ABC-CLIO, LLC
130 Cremona Drive, P.O. Box 1911
Santa Barbara, California 93116-1911

This book is printed on acid-free paper ∞

Manufactured in the United States of America

Contents

v

Foreword

It seems to me that there has long been a disconnect regarding scientific and other types of scholarly and professional publications. We have always assumed that we write for publication. In fact, in the sciences, we say that an experiment is not complete until the results have been published. Yet, in most fields most of the time, we are not really "writing for publication." We are "writing for conferences." The vast majority of the new knowledge that appears in our books and other publications does not get there until it has been "conferenced."

While reading the manuscript for this book, it dawned on me that our current attitudes regarding scholarly publication may be a bit skewed. For example, a large number of books have been written about scientific and scholarly publication (I have written a couple myself), but this book by Mallette and Berger is, I believe, the first to zero in on the primal source of our scholarly knowledge, the conference.

Sure, the published article in a peer-reviewed journal is still the coin of our realm, but we should keep in mind that the genesis of that article was almost certainly a presentation at a conference. Thus, this book, which describes the many activities that occur at the beginning of the publishing process, should be of value to many readers, especially to graduate students and young professionals.

Robert A. Day
Professor Emeritus of English at the University of
Delaware and author of *How to Write and Publish a
Scientific Paper* and *Scientific English*

Acknowledgments

We would like to extend our deepest gratitude to Pepperdine University for bringing us together in its Organizational Leadership Doctoral Program. Thanks to Dr. June Schmieder-Ramirez, who sparked our interest in writing this book when she casually mentioned, "You should write a book." As a result, *Writing for Conferences* was born. A special thanks to our friend, Leslie Ann Evans (1957–2009), who edited early drafts of several chapters.

Author Leo Mallette. I would like to thank my wife, Kathy Mallette, for her patience while writing, rewriting, and re-rewriting these chapters. Luckily, Kathy and I have taken this book's advice and have gone to many conferences together. We especially enjoyed the conferences in Besançon, France; Las Vegas, Nevada; and Hawaii. Finally, a special thank you to my co-author Clare Berger for helping make this book as good as it could be.

Author Clare Berger. It is my hope this book will launch many publishing careers. A sincere thanks to our many contributors for openly sharing their personal publishing experiences and providing valuable suggestions over the course of developing *Writing for Conferences*.

Leo Mallette and Clare Berger
writingforconferences.com

Introduction

A rule of thumb: More is always better. Not more pages, more publications. (Bucholtz 2010)

I need a job.
I want a better job.
I want a different job.
I want to do my own research.
I'd like to be a tenured professor.
I think I might want to change jobs.

If you have ever said these words to yourself, you may have tried working a heavier workload, broadening your skills at work by taking on other assignments, increasing your skills by taking classes, and maybe you have pursued another degree. These are all worthwhile accomplishments, and *Writing for Conferences* can help you reach your goals. This book is a tool you can use to add to your list of accomplishments—becoming a published author. This book is for students who have never published a scholarly paper, it is a review for more experienced writers, and it is a guide for anyone who aspires to publish, whether it is in a newsletter for your collectibles, a local newspaper, a gardening magazine, or a professional journal.

Conferences are often a researcher's first foray into publishing, and there are no books devoted to this subject. *Writing for Conferences* is unique in that it addresses conferences, and only conferences, to get you started on your publishing journey. Conferences have many more dimensions than traditional journal and book publishing, due to quick turnaround, oral presentation, immediate feedback, and the opportunity for networking. These additional dimensions are not typically discussed in other books. The purpose of this book is to help graduate students take their first steps into the publishing landscape.

There are many books on publishing for magazines and journals, how to write books, how to write books for children, how to illustrate books, why professors need to publish, and how to write dissertations. These do not prepare the writer for the total conference experience because most writing can be done without ever meeting another individual; it can be done by mail and e-mail. Whereas writing for a conference also includes preparation of a presentation, physical presentation of your subject to peers, and answering questions about your topic. There is a greater amount of interaction with other human beings, the immediate feedback from your peers, and one of the best opportunities to network.

This cross-disciplinary book on conference publishing helps you navigate one aspect of the publication landscape and is intended to be used as a reference by any master's or doctoral graduate student. *Writing for Conferences* would be a useful text for qualitative and quantitative research methods classes, as well as final dissertation research classes. In addition, this book augments existing texts and provides a clear path to publishing. An instructor could assign this text, walk away, and a student would be taken through the processes needed to publish a conference paper.

In the *Guide to the Successful Thesis and Dissertation,* the authors state, "High quality research should be characterized by publication" (Mauch and Birch 1998, 15). Every dissertation should be publishable, and *Writing for Conferences* will help students make the jump into conference publishing. Some schools require the findings of dissertation research be published as part of the matriculation process, and this book is poised to fill the void created by this requirement. According to the *ProQuest Dissertations and Theses* database, approximately 50,000 doctoral candidates graduate every year. Table 0.1 highlights the number of doctoral degrees posted on that database in the last two decades. Note that the last year or two may be incomplete, due to degrees that have not yet been added to the database.

TABLE 0.1
Number of Doctorates in the Last Two Decades

Year	Total	Year	Total	Year	Total	Year	Total
1990	48,130	1995	52,550	2000	52,831	2005	53,540
1991	48,903	1996	52,983	2001	51,472	2006	55,150
1992	48,279	1997	55,033	2002	51,256	2007	56,642
1993	49,225	1998	53,201	2003	51,895	2008	53,952
1994	51,527	1999	52,519	2004	52,766	2009	52,156

Source: *ProQuest Dissertations and Theses* database

Since this book is cross-disciplinary, it can be used in many areas outside of academia, including businesses, government entities, and nonprofit organizations that encourage employees to publish at conferences. Companies and organizations that sponsor conferences could provide this book to their employees, constituents, and suppliers who will be attending their conferences.

Writing for Conferences will prepare you for every aspect of a conference. It speaks to graduate students in an informal style, providing many examples to show good and bad experiences, and explains how to make the most of this opportunity for professional growth. This book is a guide for previously unpublished students. The treatment is practical, and the approach is distinctive.

The authors have studied and applied andragogical methods in developing this manual that are intended for adult learners who want to learn what is needed to publish at a conference. The information in some chapters may seem quite basic, but the authors found that unpublished students ask these questions. Case studies from the literature and authors' experiences will be used to aid the reader with practical advice. Vignettes from many different published authors highlighting their first experiences and worksheets to aid students in planning the many phases of the project will be included. Although this book could be used as a primary text for a dissertation or research class, this book is not meant as a primary text, but as a supplement.

Writing for Conferences also will serve as a guide for graduate students who want to publish research projects. The book is a reference guide on scholarly writing, ethics in publishing, and networking to develop further research and career opportunities. The authors use a humorous style to discuss topics such as how to choose the right conference, the timeline of important events, budgeting expenses, and presentation tips. The authors include case studies, examples, vignettes, sidebars highlighting special topics, definitions when first used in the text and in a glossary, worksheets, and some what-if scenarios.

Writing for Conferences follows the timeline of a conference paper. Section I asks the question: *What's in it for me?* It answers the question by discussing why you would want to publish at a conference instead of another venue, what it will cost, and publishing statistics.

Section II walks you through the steps needed to select the right conference for your topic. It addresses how to find out about upcoming conferences, how to read a call for papers, and the timeline for submitting a paper to a conference.

Section III describes first steps by discussing solo authorship versus multiple authorship, finding co-authors, the abstract submission process, and a few vignettes from the authors' experiences with publishing conference papers and how they were conceived.

Finally, Section IV discusses scholarly writing and preparation of presentations for conferences. It includes the topic of social interaction at conferences, how to be a session chair, and suggests that conferences are one of the ultimate networking events.

Bibliography

Bucholtz, Mary. "Tips for Academic Publishing," http://www.linguistics. ucsb.edu/faculty/bucholtz/sociocultural/publishingtips.html (cited August 1, 2010).

Mauch, James, and Jack Birch. *Guide to the Successful Thesis and Dissertation: Conception to Publication; A Handbook for Students and Faculty.* New York: Marcel Dekker, 1998.

ProQuest Dissertations and Theses Database, http://proquest.umi.com.lib. pepperdine.edu/pqdweb?RQT=302&COPT=REJTPTNiMGYmSU5 UPTAmVkVSPTI=&clientId=1686&cfc=1 (cited October 6, 2007).

Section I

Introduction to Publishing at Conferences

This section discusses the reasons for choosing to publish at conferences versus in journals or magazines. It also addresses questions about costs and publishing rates. The chapters are

1. Why Do I Want to Publish at a Conference?
2. Why a Conference and Not a Magazine?
3. How Much Will It Cost Me?
4. What Are the Statistics of Publishing?

Chapter 1 reviews the advantages of publishing a paper at a conference and includes the benefits of presentation and networking. Chapter 2 points out differences between conference publication and other forms of publication and discusses the advantages of each. Chapter 3 addresses the costs of attending a conference, including opportunity costs, significant other travel, and hidden costs. The final chapter in Section I presents some statistics and a challenge to the reader. Let's get started by talking about why you might want to publish the work you are doing.

Opportunities for professional advancement await those with the ambition and expertise needed to write for conferences. (Dreamstime.com)

I

Advantages of Conference Publishing

You must direct the reader to focus on what they want to be known for in academic circles. (Ray Valadez, personal communication, August 21, 2007)

Introduction

Have you thought about changing jobs? Do you aspire to higher levels at your current job? Have you considered teaching? Do you want to consult for organizations? Have you always wondered whether you could write for publication? Do you long to share your ideas with others?

Publishing at a conference can give you those opportunities. Publishing your work brands you as an expert in a topic and gives you credibility you can parlay into a multitude of advantages. Publishing will help to dramatically further your professional and personal goals. After reading this book, you will understand how easy it can be to become a published author.

What Are My Professional Goals?

Professional goals that can be furthered by publishing at conferences often fall into three categories: business, academia, and consulting. Whereas each category has its own needs, they all have something in common—you can use publishing to brand yourself as a subject matter expert. Branding can easily be accomplished by selecting the appropriate topic and sharing your research with the scholarly community that attends conferences. Dr. Ray Valadez, one of the vignette contributors to this book, stated it this way:

> You must direct the reader to focus on what they want to be known for in academic circles. In other words, what is their passion? I find that there are so many conferences and calls for papers that it may be a bit overwhelming to try to publish and present on different subjects. Knowing what you are passionate about and becoming an expert in that field should give you the self confidence to tackle the publication. (Valadez, personal communication, August 21, 2007)

Whether you are in business, academia, or consulting, publishing a book or articles in journals and at conferences is good for your brand.

Business

Most people in business are thinking one of two thoughts: either they are dreaming about changing jobs, or they are dreaming of getting promoted. Either path requires that you be branded as capable, knowledgeable, and dynamic. The presentation skills you develop by presenting papers at conferences can prepare you to excel in your current job or allow you to develop expertise in a new area. This, in turn, will allow you to transition into a new field or to a new company within your field.

In addition to honing your presentation skills, you will automatically become a published author: Almost every conference publishes what is called *conference proceedings,* a collection of all papers presented at a conference. Colleagues consult published articles from conference proceedings for subsequent reference in future research projects. Recent conference proceedings are typically published in the form of CDs rather than printed and are either given out at the conference to registered participants or mailed to registered participants after the conference.

Conference Lingo

Conference proceedings (or digest) is a collection of all papers that were presented at a conference.

In addition to conference proceedings, occasionally peer-reviewed journals will accept your conference paper for consideration, especially if you have presented the paper and have had the opportunity to incorporate constructive comments into your first version. Publication in a peer-reviewed journal is a helpful opportunity to receive feedback on your writing from experts in the field. Typically, one to three reviewers knowledgeable in the subject matter read and critique your submission. If it is of the quality the journal requires and would add valuable information to the journal's readership, your paper will be accepted for publication. Being published in a peer-reviewed journal is definitely a prized notch in your belt. (Journals and magazines are discussed further in Chapter 2.)

Getting published at a conference adds credibility to your brand as a subject matter expert and gives you constructive experience in presenting your ideas to a scholarly audience. Such experiences give you a competitive advantage that is hard to match when you apply for a new job or seek that promotion that you have been dreaming about.

Academia

Have you ever considered teaching? Many graduate students find teaching a natural extension of their years as a learner, even after ten or fifteen years in business. Some feel a passion to make a difference in the educational field they have come to love. Others want to contribute to the academic community or share their knowledge. No matter what motivates you to consider academia as a profession or even as a part-time endeavor, entering the field requires experience with presenting information in front of a group. Presenting your work at conferences is an excellent learning opportunity and gives you hands-on experience in a classroom-like setting. Most conference presentations are very similar to presenting one of your class projects to fellow students.

Your university is considered either a research-type or a teaching-type university (or some combination of both). Generally, in the United States, research-type universities tend to be called *University of (name of state),* whereas teaching-type universities tend to be called *(name of state) State University.* Your paper topic may be oriented toward pure research or may be targeted to practitioner conferences. (Types of conferences will be discussed further in Chapter 6.)

> **Hint**
>
> Choose your conferences carefully, as they will help shape your brand.

In addition to the skills you develop in presenting, publication is looked upon favorably when you try to make the leap into the educational arena. Most schools (typically research-based institutions) require professors to publish. Some schools have guidelines that define or recommend how many publications per year they require of their faculty to gain tenure. (Caution: These guidelines usually refer to publications in peer-reviewed journals.) Publication guidelines will vary by the type of university and the research ranking of the department. Whether publication credit is required or just highly regarded, you can earn publication credit by presenting at conferences. And one of the best things you can do for your curriculum vitae (CV) is to add a list of your publication credits.

Curriculum vitae is Latin for "course of life." Accordingly, a CV generally lists your education, experience, publications, presentations, committees, and associations. A summary CV is usually limited to one page, but a full CV with a list of all publications and classes taught can be well over ten pages. An outline of a CV is given in Appendix 1A.

Consulting

Have you ever considered becoming an organizational consultant? Consulting can offer many career advantages from flexibility to good pay to freedom from tyrannical bosses. Consulting for organizations requires a demonstrated level of expertise in a field. After all, why should a company pay you to come in and advise them on how to manage their company or their technical problem? What credibility do you have? Are you a known expert with a track record? Publishing your work at a conference can provide validation that you are indeed a subject matter expert. Your ideas will have been considered and discussed by experts and other interested parties in the field. Conferences are an excellent place to network for future business and also provide a testing ground for your new ideas. There are conferences for every field of endeavor, whether your interests lie in

---

Definition

Curriculum vitae (CV or vitae) is the type of resume used in some creative fields, including academia. In addition to the typical entries found on a resume, a CV includes sections for publications, presentations, and professional activities. Latin for "course of life."

---

education, business, engineering, human resource management, global humanitarian efforts…the list is almost endless.

Finding work as a consultant requires that you brand yourself as knowledgeable in your area of expertise. Publishing several papers on a particular topic helps reinforce your brand in that specialized field. Your brand can be crafted by the type of conferences you choose and the topics you decide to write about. Figure 1.1 is a checklist of possible professional and personal goals that you can use to guide your conference choices (more in Chapter 6). Fill it out now, or at least start thinking about your responses to this checklist.

Professional Goals
1. Promotion to
2.
3.
Personal Goals
1. Travel to
2.
3.
Reasons why people want to hear what I have to say:
1. Some of the stuff I do is really interesting.
2.
3.

Figure 1.1.
Checklist of Possible Professional and Personal Goals

What Are My Personal Goals?

Have you dreamed of being known as an expert in your field of endeavor? Do you have a desire to share your knowledge and passion with others? Do you enjoy learning new things and meeting new people? Do you want to create a personal network? Do you like to explore new places? Conferences are a great way to expand your network, develop relationships with other like-minded learners, and may provide an opportunity to travel. Some ways to achieve these goals are described in more detail in the following sections.

Branding

Publishing is an effective way to create a brand for yourself that can shape your image, improve your self-confidence, and push your credibility index higher as a subject matter expert. Moreover, publishing can identify you as knowledgeable in a specific area and create a competitive advantage in your next job search.

Share My Knowledge

Giving back to others can be rewarding. Creating a legacy by sharing your wealth of knowledge is made possible whenever you present at conferences. Even beyond the conference itself, the knowledge published from your research will remain in the scholarly annals to be accessed by future learners. Conference presentations also afford an opportunity to document your work or intermediate progress on a longer project or to update work done on a previously published study.

Gain Knowledge

One common personal goal is to enhance your skills and knowledge base. Participating in conferences allows you to share your ideas with other interested parties. There is usually a discussion of your work, whether formal or informal, that helps you to clarify new areas to research, fine-tune your existing premises, or initiate future collaborations. Your investment of time and money in conference publications usually pays off handsomely in keeping your skill set relevant.

Expand My Network

There are many networking opportunities at conferences; networking is expanded upon in Chapter 14. Opportunities to network, such as meals and an exhibits area, are built into the agenda and events of many conferences. Often, people will approach you after hearing your presentation to ask more detailed questions. Sometimes they ask to exchange business cards with you to follow up later on a future collaboration. Some preliminary steps in a job offer may be shared. Networking is critical and will affect you throughout your career. The relationships you form during conferences can be of value to you for a lifetime.

Explore New Places

If you love to travel, publishing at conferences can be a great way to travel to locations that you have only dreamed about. The location should not be your primary purpose for attending a conference, but there are conferences on many topics in almost every corner of the globe. Do you have a favorite city you enjoy visiting? Do you want an excuse to visit relatives for an evening? Sometimes the conference expenses are reimbursable from your employer or educational institution. This is one way to see another part of the country or the world, subsidized by your company or university.

Develop Relationships with Other Learners

The people you meet at conferences are generally learners who enjoy seeking knowledge just as you do. They bring a scholarly interest to discussions and are generally willing to help by providing information and contacts for additional resources. Scholars interested in getting assistance on thesis projects or dissertations can often find other experts in the field who are willing to be contacted to give guidance or answer questions. If you take the time to network at conferences, you can develop continuing relationships that will benefit you in many ways and for many years. One of the authors had co-authored a paper with another expert in the field but had not worked with him. They were not with the same company, and they worked 3,000 miles apart. The two co-authors found themselves working on the same project nine years later and, because of the earlier

> **Hint**
>
> Plan to spend part of the week following the conference on following up with contacts made there. When receiving a business card from someone, take a moment to write some information about the person and what they are interested in on the back of the card to guide you in your follow-up.

collaboration, enjoyed an excellent working relationship from the first moment of the initial meeting on the new project.

Why Would They Be Interested in What I Have to Say?

There are many reasons why conference-goers would be interested in what you have to say. Every individual comes to a situation with a wealth of life experience and a unique perspective. Those who seek knowledge enjoy hearing about the experiences of others. The basic tenets of adult learning are wanting to learn, basing learning on personal experience, and needing to be relevant immediately. Conferences can satisfy all these requirements.

Specific Knowledge

You probably have specific professional knowledge of your industry or field of interest that others would be interested in knowing. Through your conference writings, you have a chance to share knowledge with a wider circle of individuals, influencing many more people than you would typically come into contact with, even people from other continents. Successive generations could be influenced by your thoughts.

Experiential Knowledge

Your life has been filled with experiences that are uniquely yours. There are people who would be interested in hearing about your experiences. Perhaps you have traveled to exotic locations and can describe the culture and customs of the region. Perhaps you have experienced the pain of addiction and recovery and have meaningful experiences that could help others. Experiential knowledge is a good starting point for expressing your views.

Practical Applications

One easy way to get published is to write about a practical application or process that made a difference in your workplace. Many people are anxious to hear scenarios or case studies about what has worked in other organizations with the hope that they can glean new insight to make their jobs easier or to create change within their organizations.

People Are Interested in Passion—They Are Drawn to It

If you are passionate about a topic, write about it. People are naturally drawn to those who express passion for their work. Passion will drive you and create a dynamic presentation that will generate a lot of audience buzz. This buzz can turn into networking opportunities as people come forward to hear more details about your topic.

Summary

Why should you publish at a conference? This venue allows you to share your research faster than publishing in a journal, provides a chance to practice presentations with immediate feedback, and creates an opportunity for networking. This type of publishing is a relatively easy way to accomplish many of your professional and personal goals. Whether you are interested in business, academia, or consulting, you can create a competitive advantage by publishing at conferences. You have something to say that is worth communicating. Sharing your knowledge with others can be a very satisfying experience. By following the tips in this book, you can master the art of getting published and fulfill some of your dreams.

Appendix 1A

Outline of a Multipage Curriculum Vitae

(Your Name)
Your Current Title, School of xxx
Mailing Address: E-mail: xxx
Xxx Washington Street, Anytown, State, Zip

Education:
PhD   (discipline and school)
Minor: xxx
Dissertation: (title)

M.A.   (discipline and school)
M.B.A.   (discipline and school)
B.A.   (discipline and school)

Teaching Service:
Professor–September 2002 to present, school
Associate Professor–September 1997 to August 2002, school
Assistant Professor–September 1991 to June 1997, school

Courses Taught at xxx University:
List classes

Dissertations Chaired
Over xxx dissertations chaired. Selected dissertations:
Students, year, title

Publications:

Books:
List using appropriate format for your discipline

Book Chapters:
List using appropriate format for your discipline

Book Reviews:
List using appropriate format for your discipline

Books in Progress:
List using appropriate format for your discipline

(Selected) Articles:
List all (or selected) peer-reviewed journal articles using appropriate
    format

Articles in Progress:
List peer-reviewed journal articles using appropriate format, if needed

Presentations:

Published Proceedings:
List published papers from conferences using appropriate format for your
   discipline

Presentations:
List conference presentations and other significant presentations using
   appropriate format

Administrative and Leadership:

Academic Positions:
List

Credentials/Certifications:
List

Grants/Funded Programs
List. This category should be more prominently placed for a research-in-
   tensive university.

Professional Memberships
List

Special Honors
List

Industrial Experience:
List work in industry as employee, consultant, manager, owner, and
   so on

References:
Reference #1 with phone number and e-mail
Reference #2 with phone number and e-mail
Reference #3 with phone number and e-mail

One of the first steps is to weigh the advantages of writing for conferences versus writing for other publications. (iStockphoto.com)

2

Conferences versus Other Forms of Publishing

Conference advantages: the presentation, the immediate feedback from peers, and the ability to network.

Introduction

Although the authors focus on publishing for conferences, there are several different ways for you to publish if you would like to branch out. Journal articles, magazines, association newsletters, books, and even blogging are avenues you can use to get published. Choosing a path for publishing really depends on your goals and purpose, items you previously reflected upon in Chapter 1. This chapter will briefly introduce various venues in the publishing landscape and then will discuss how conferences are similar to or different from the other publishing venues.

Definition: Publishing Landscape

The environment in which you can publish. The publishing landscape includes conferences, journals, books (fiction, nonfiction, romance, travel, cooking, children's, etc.), magazines, book reviews, newspapers, letters to the editor, and online sites such as Web sites, blogs, diaries, and so on.

Conferences and Other Venues

The publishing landscape can include many different venues, and each has advantages.

Conference Articles

Conferences offer budding authors and researchers an opportunity to distribute their work to attendees of the conference and anyone that can get a copy of the conference digest. These digests are often distributed to libraries in the professional area associated with the conference. For example, Lockheed-Martin may obtain copies of engineering conferences, and Children's Hospital of Orange County may get copies of medical and nursing conferences. The disadvantages include high cost and limited distribution. Online databases are getting better every year.

Journal Articles

Peer-reviewed journal articles are the most important type of publishing for tenure-seeking professors. Publications in the top-tier journals in your field are like gold medals at the Olympics. Similar to conferences, journal articles also involve preparing an abstract and meeting deadlines; however, you do not have to travel to get your article published. If you are inexperienced with publishing journal articles, the authors recommend you seek out one of your professors to see if he or she might be interested in co-authoring a journal article with you. Study various journals to find a suitable match for your article and review the past 5 to 20 years of the journal for articles similar to yours that can become part of your literature search. If there are no similar articles, it may not be the best journal for your article. The major advantage of publishing in a peer-reviewed journal is the prestige. These publications are valuable for assistant professors that are attempting to become tenured. The disadvantages are the need for thick skin because acceptance rates can be quite low and receiving a negative review or an outright rejection can be

---

Reviewers Can Be Brutal with Their Red Pens

"I thought he had ritually sacrificed some small animal over it." (Clapham 2005)

devastating. Do not be discouraged; you can learn from negative reviews, sometimes allowing you to turn your article into a publishable one.

Magazines

Magazines provide you an opportunity to publish lighter material and non-academic material. You don't have to leave your home or office, cite references, or ground your theories in pages of research information. You might even be able to get paid for a magazine article.

Association Newsletters

Publishing an article in an appropriate association newsletter is a convenient way to ease into publishing nonacademic material for the first timer. You probably have one of these on your desk. Again, find an appropriate match for your article. For example, if you've written a political article, chances are it is not a good fit for a training newsletter.

Books

Books are an excellent way to publish a large amount of information on a single topic. There are a myriad of books to be found that describe how to write books, find a publisher, and market your book. They can be self-published or published by a full-service publisher. There can be a stigma attached to self-publishing a book, and you should read the literature and get professional advice before self-publishing your book. Some of the disadvantages of writing a book are that they are a lot of work, take a lot of time, and are expensive. If you are publishing an academic text with a small market, you may never recover the opportunity costs for the personal time you spent writing the book. You have to have a passion for the subject (think back to your dissertation or thesis) and remember the years you had to maintain your passion for the subject. The primary author of this book has published articles at conferences from France to Hawaii since 1978—he has a passion for publishing.

Blogging

Blogging is becoming quite popular. Although it is not an official way to publish, if you are blogging, your blog is available to the public. This is great for editorial comments and publicity, but not for scholarly research.

Newspapers

Feel free to publish your opinion on any topic in an op-ed article, but newspapers are not the best way of publishing scholarly research.

Conference Differences

The advantages to publishing for a conference are the presentation, the immediate feedback from peers, and the ability to network. There is also a possible increase in credibility and respect. However, a poorly written article or a bad presentation can lead to loss of credibility and respect. Since conferences are held in various places and the digest of papers often has limited distribution, you have the ability to publish similar but significantly modified papers at different conferences. The following paragraphs describe the unique properties of conferences.

Time Consumption and Cost

There are some negative aspects—conferences take a lot of time. In addition to researching and writing the paper, you will have to prepare a presentation, travel to the conference site, and show up for the entire conference or at least your session. It could be considered a waste of time. Most conference program committees accept your paper based on only a review of the abstract. This could lead to low quality work. You could also be presenting to an audience of only three people if the conference has low

---

SIDEBAR

Leo Milked His Master's Thesis

A friend once stated that one of the authors *milked* his master's thesis. He worked on the project and the thesis writing for many months, but he also published three conference articles based on different parts of the research performed during those months.

attendance, or if there are parallel sessions and the other sessions are more interesting. It could be that your topic is not a good fit for a conference, or it could be the coordinator's fault—there could also be a lack of breadth of submissions or too much breadth. There could also be the problem that your session is in conflict with other events. Another driving factor is that the conference may be held in an undesirable location or could be overpriced. All of these are negative factors to consider.

Networking and Employment

Conferences provide the opportunity for networking. This could be a problem if you are antisocial, more of an introvert, and just don't feel a need to talk to others in your field. Many people may be shy or antisocial, but most people don't fall into the latter category. Even shy individuals can practice and spend a few moments at a conference interacting with peers, learning new ideas, and sharing their ideas with others.

Bring business cards to the conference. You can have them made a few weeks before the conference. You can even get them for free—do a search on the Internet for free business cards. You may have to pay for shipping, but it's normally a small cost. When you receive a business card, write a note on the back about the other person. You might want to follow up with an idea for a co-authored paper, comment on a book they recommended, note that they wanted you to send them a reference they needed, a good restaurant recommendation, or it might be a lead for a potential job.

A potential new job is interesting to all of us. It's the chance to see the greener grass in another company or to try a different type of employment opportunity, such as working in government, a community college, a university, an industry, a new start-up, as a postdoctoral fellow, for a nonprofit, or as a volunteer. The opportunity for an increase in salary or to qualify for a bonus plan is often incentive enough.

Networking applies to undergraduate and graduate students who are about to enter the workforce and start paying off their student loans. Being known in an industry, knowing a few people in your potential next employer's company, and knowing what they published is valuable during the interview process.

Knowing What He Published

Joe Pifko, Integrated Product Team Leader

My present assignment was ending. I had an interview scheduled with a potential new boss, so it was essential to make a good impression and pass the interview. In preparation for the interview, I went to Google to determine if there was any information on this person. The search resulted in learning that the potential boss had a PhD in mathematics from UCLA, so I knew that I should not mention my daughter's recent graduation from USC (a rival school). I also learned that the new boss's dissertation was on a very specialized mathematical tool. I continued the search to get additional information on this tool. During the interview, I managed to work into one of my answers that I might have an opportunity to use this specialized tool in a potential analysis. The reaction was one of amazement that this expert might be helpful in working with his potential new employee. Needless to say, I got the job. ■

Learning

Conferences are a two-way process—you presenting to them, and them presenting to you. There will be interesting sessions with fascinating topics, and there will be plenty that will put you to sleep. Don't get caught dozing during a presentation; it's embarrassing for the presenter and you. If it's a boring paper, attend one of the more interesting parallel sessions or go outside and network. Learning from the other presenters at the conference may generate new ideas and interests. It also may lead to collaboration with others for your next paper.

Diversity of Learning

Similar to parallel sessions at one conference, there may be multiple simultaneous conferences that can be attended with only one registration. An example of this is the excerpt from a call for papers in the sidebar Conjoined Conferences.

SIDEBAR

Conjoined Conferences

The International Symposium on Design and Research in the Artificial and the Natural Sciences: DRANS 2010 was organized in the context of The 14th World Multi-Conference on Systemics, Cybernetics and Informatics: WMSCI 2010 in Orlando, Florida. The deadline for DRANS 2010 is April 14, 2010. You can also submit your abstract to another area or to any of the following conjoined events:

- The SUMMER 4th International Conference on Knowledge Generation, Communication and Management: KGCM 2010
- The 3rd International Symposium on Academic Globalization: AG 2010
- The 2nd International Symposium on Peer Reviewing: ISPR 2010
- The 3rd International Multi-Conference on Engineering and Technological Innovation: IMETI 2010

The preceding text was extracted from an e-mail from drans@ mail.sysconfer.org, received on March 22, 2010 (Web sites and some text removed).

Summary

This chapter introduced various venues in scholarly publishing landscape, such as conferences, journals, magazines, and books. The last half of the chapter discussed how conferences are similar or different from the other publishing venues. The major differences between conferences and other publishing venues are the ability to quickly present your research, get feedback, network with peers, and possibly provide an interesting place to visit.

Bibliography

Clapham, Phil. "Publish or Perish." *Bioscience* 55 (5) (2005): 390–391.

An inevitable part of attending conferences is the cost for travel, as well as for registration, hotels, and meals. (Dreamstime.com)

3

Expected Costs of Conference Publishing

You need to ask yourself if you really want to pay $300 to $1,500 to publish this paper.

Introduction

You might wonder (if you have an inflated ego) how much you would get paid to present a paper. After all, you get paid to go to work, so you should get paid to go to a conference.

Right?

No. Not really.

In addition to implicitly agreeing to attend and present a paper, you will have to pay for the privilege of presenting your idea. At some point during the decision process (see Chapter 6), to write a paper for a conference, you have to ask yourself two questions:

1. How much will this conference cost?

2. Who will pay for it?

Regardless of who pays for it, the first part of this process is to understand the costs. Your employer will want to know, in order to verify they are within budget, and you want to know for the same reason: Can you afford it? You have to consider direct conference costs such as transportation, parking costs at the airport, food, hotel, and registration. You also have to

> **SIDEBAR**
>
> **Ethics**
>
> If you submit a paper, you are committing yourself to attending and presenting that paper.

consider the not-so-direct costs, such as your time away from work, what to do with pets, what clothes you might have to buy for the conference, and roaming charges on your cell phone. What are the costs of your significant other going with you? After all, most conferences are held in interesting places. Conversely, what are the costs of your significant other not going with you? Souvenirs or gifts to show you were thinking of him or her are items that will increase the cost of the conference. There are also opportunity costs to consider (What else could I be doing with my time, instead of preparing and going to the conference?) such as being with the family, taking a class, exercising, working longer at work, or attending a child's recital. Let's begin by discussing the direct costs of the conference.

Direct Costs

The authors chose to address the conference costs (in the next section) in the order in which they will need to be paid. For example, you will always need to register for the conference, and there will always be some travel costs incurred, even if it is a local conference.

Registration

The cost of attending the conference will always be required. This is usually called the "registration fee" and is often based on the number of days in the conference and what is included (e.g., meals, transportation, keynote speakers, etc). It is safe to assume that the registration fee will be $100–$200 for each day of the conference. So a four-day conference would cost at least $400. There are specialized conferences that may charge more for registration, and cost-of-living increases may drive the daily rate to $150 per day in the near future. The cost of the conference will be higher if meals are included.

Registration Mishap—Surprise!

One of the authors registered early for a conference, paid by credit card, and received an electronic confirmation. Luckily, this normally unorganized author brought the online confirmation with him to the conference. He arrived and found he was not registered. Surprise! The registration people scrambled for a few minutes and eventually had to on-site register but were able to get the early registration price because he had his confirmation. He checked the credit card bills upon returning home and, indeed, the first registration never happened. He never did find out why the original credit card transaction was never consummated. ■

Tutorials, also known as workshops, are optional and are often held before, during, or after a conference. There may be a cost per tutorial or per day or for an entire package of tutorials. These are important if your industry requires annual training and a minimum of three or six continuing education units (CEU). The costs for tutorials will vary from $40 per tutorial to over $200 for an entire day of tutorials. Tutorials are meant to inform the registrants. Tutorials, if offered, are always an option in the registration package. Two examples of typical registration fees are given in Figures 3.1 and 3.2.

Travel

The second required cost is travel. Whether the conference is around the corner from your house or in Budapest, there will be some travel costs involved. A local conference may include only the cost of your gas and the parking at the hotel. A not-so-local conference will usually include parking

---

Registration Hint

Don't forget to look and ask for the early bird, student, senior, or retired discount on registration—or you may only need to attend the conference for one day.

Conference Fees (Select Full or Daily Registration)				
	Full Registration On or Before May 16	Full Registration After May 16	Daily Registration On or Before May 16	Daily Registration After May 16	Enclosed
Member	$325	$425	$225	$325	$_____
New/Renewing Member	$375	$475	$275	$325	$_____
Nonmember	$375	$475	$275	$325	$_____
Student Member (without proceedings)	$125	$125	$125	$125	$_____
Disabled Member (without proceedings)	$125	$125	$125	$125	$_____

Figure 3.1.
Typical Registration Costs for a Conference

Conference Activity	Price
Attendee Registration Fee—Early Bird (received before September 1st)	$385
Attendee Registration Fee—Regular (received on or after September 1st)	$435
Attendee Registration Fee—Walk-In Price	$585
One day—Tuesday only	$200
One day—Wednesday only	$200
One day—Thursday only	$200
One day—Friday only	$150
Doctoral Student Forum	Free
Monday golf tournament (includes cart rental)	$45 per person
Monday Tutorials	$145
Tuesday evening luau	$42
Wednesday evening awards banquet	$60
Friday tour of XYZ facility	$18
Breakfast for speakers only	Speakers, on day of presentation only, free
Lunch package (4 days in Plaza Ballroom A)	$80

Figure 3.2.
Typical Registration Costs for Another Conference

> **Travel Hint**
>
> Don't overlook your frequent-flier miles when planning your conference.
>   The best airfare is free airfare!

at the airport, airfare, and taxi or car rental in the destination city. You will know that your paper has been accepted a few months ahead of time and will be able to book the lowest airfare. You can assume you will pay $200 to $700 for a 21-day advance purchase, nonrefundable, economy class airline ticket within the United States. The price will vary depending on distance, carrier, location of the destination city, and any special fares that the airlines might offer. International travel can be much more expensive.

Other travel-related costs are listed in Table 3.1 and may include your personal car mileage (to cover gas, insurance, and depreciation), parking costs when you get to the airport (this can be $10 to $30 per day), parking costs at the conference hotel (whether you drive yourself or rent a car and park at the hotel), and taxi, shuttle, or car rental costs at the destination city.

Hotel

The cost of the hotel may be zero if it is a local conference or if you have nearby relatives that you can impose upon. Hotels will usually offer negotiated lower rates for conferences that are held in their hotel. You can often get lower rates at nearby hotels that are not at the conference location, because they are not on the beach or right on Las Vegas Boulevard. However, if you are debating whether to stay at the conference's hotel or at a more affordable hotel that is a block away, keep in mind that it is very convenient to be able to run up to your room between papers to grab some aspirin, brush your teeth after lunch, change your clothes if you spilled your lunch on them, do a quick check of your e-mail, and even catch a five-minute nap. You might decide that the extra costs of staying at the conference hotel outweigh the inconvenience of being at another hotel for a few dollars less per night. Room rates of $100 to $200 per night are common. You can cut this in half if you share a room with someone. You can estimate your other hotel-related costs by using the checklist in Table 3.1.

TABLE 3.1
Checklist of Possible Conference Costs

Registration
Registration .... $_____
Banquet ticket .... $_____
Awards luncheon .... $_____
Tutorials .... $_____
Social events .... $_____

Travel
Personal car mileage .... $_____
Parking at airport .... $_____
Airline ticket .... $_____
Taxi or shuttle at destination city .... $_____
Toll charges .... $_____
Car rental: __ days at $_____ per day .... $_____
Other (gas, insurance, etc.) .... $_____

Hotel
__ nights at $_____ per night .... $_____
State tax .... $_____
Local bed or occupancy taxes .... $_____
Parking at conference hotel .... $_____
Phone calls .... $_____
Other (movies, mini bar, etc.) .... $_____

Meals (not covered by the conference)
__ breakfasts x __ days at $_____ per breakfast .... $_____
__ lunches x __ days at $_____ per lunch .... $_____
__ dinners x __ days at $_____ per dinner .... $_____
Other (bar tab, meals for associates, snacks, etc.) .... $_____

Extras
Significant other travel costs .... $_____
Golf package .... $_____
Tours .... $_____
Tourist items (t-shirts, gifts for family or coworkers, etc.) ...... $_____
Other .... $_____

Total .... $_____

Hotel Hint

Don't forget to look or ask for any special rates or discounts that hotels might offer (conference, AAA, online, military, corporate, student, and senior discounts).

Meals

Conferences sometimes provide breakfasts or lunches as part of the registration fee—sometimes the breakfasts are just for presenters on the day of their presentation. Meals serve the dual purposes of providing convenience for the participants and allows for a congenial venue for scholarly exchanges with your peers. You can sit with people you know and get updated on their activities since last year, or you can sit with an individual or group that you don't know and learn who they are and what they are doing. You may seek out a particular presenter from an earlier session to sit with and discuss how his topic might apply to your situation. And, vice versa, someone may seek you (the famous presenter) after you present your paper. Please be cordial to people who seem to be approaching you with a question. Many conferences also have a formal lunch or dinner banquet that may include award presentations, a keynote presenter, and maybe music. If the conference does not offer meals, you have the option of eating in your room, eating at the hotel restaurant, finding a fast food place, or finding a nice restaurant at which to leisurely eat. You also have the option to not eat—this may work if you had a hearty breakfast at home and plan to be back home for dinner. However, you should plan for meals at a

---

SIDEBAR

Should I Stay at the Conference Hotel?

Keep in mind that it is very convenient to be able to run up to your room between papers to grab some aspirin, to brush your teeth after lunch, or to do a quick update to your slides.

---

conference. Only you know your eating habits and needs. It would be safe to assume between $20 and $100 per person per day for meals.

Opportunity Cost of Cheap Meals

You can keep a stash of beef jerky in your room and get by very cheaply, but an important part of the conference experience is the business and networking that often goes on at meals. You will miss out on many of the positive social consequences of conferences if you eat in your room. See Chapter 14 for more details on networking. You also miss the opportunity to make jokes about the ubiquitous conference chicken. Stepping across the street to a fast food place is very acceptable, especially if you ask someone to go with you. This is important for networking because you never want to eat alone at a conference—see the conference networking technique called the *deep bump;* discussed throughout the book *Never Eat Alone* by Ferrazzi and Raz (2005).

Other Possible Costs

Another cost to consider is the cost of your significant other. This is discussed in detail in a subsequent section. Conferences occasionally have a team-building event that is held usually before or after the conference papers are presented. It could be a tour to a local facility of interest to the conference participants, entertainment, or a golf event. There may also be a special dinner with local entertainment (i.e., a luau or a boat cruise). Be sure to budget for these costs as well because they may not be reimbursed or included in the registration fee.

The final item you will want to plan for is the tourist items. These are the T-shirts that you bring back for yourself or your kids, a gift for your significant other or your co-author(s), a bag of locally made candies for your coworkers, or a guitar pin from the local Hard Rock Café for your neighbor who let you borrow his chain saw last April.

Nomenclature

Chicken served at conferences is often referred to as *Conference Chicken.*

Indirect Costs

This section is to remind you that there are other costs not necessarily tied to the conference that you might incur if you attend a conference.

Work Time

Your time away from work will have to be covered. You will have to take unpaid leave, or vacation time, or perhaps your time away from work will be covered in your company's overhead budget. The overhead budget (in most well-run companies) is strictly reviewed, controlled, and may not be available for conferences. You will have to find someone to cover your meetings or teaching assignments while you are gone. Remember, if they covered for you, you may have to cover for them in return someday. One of the authors has found that volunteering to take vacation time is a strong incentive for a company to pay for the registration, hotel, and transportation. However, there may be issues (i.e., insurance coverage) with being on vacation while on company business (the conference). The authors' advice is to check with your supervisor or the human resources (HR) department prior to making plans to attend the conference to ensure that you adhere to your organization's travel procedures.

Work time is less of an issue if you are a full-time student. The issue here is missing classes. Most professors can be quite sympathetic if you are publishing at a conference—especially if one of your professor is attending the same conference!

Cost of Clothing

The conference may require a different set of clothes. Jeans and flip-flops are never acceptable at conferences. The dress requirements for conferences are discussed in Chapter 12: You may have to budget for some professional clothing. You may also need to buy appropriate clothes for the weather if the conference is held in a different climate from your own. For example, you may need to buy a coat and gloves if you are a Miami native traveling to a conference in Minneapolis in February, or you may want to buy some aloha shirts if you live in the Garden State and are going to a conference in Hawaii.

SIDEBAR

Significant Other

The authors use the term *significant other* or *spouse* throughout this chapter. This term can apply to anyone who could become your conference traveling companion, such as your husband, wife, partner, friend, companion, roommate, office mate, child, parent, sibling, and so on.

Children and Pets

If you have children or pets, you may need to find someone to care for them while you attend the conference. If your significant other attends the conference location with you, she or he can watch your children. If your children must remain home, you will need to arrange for dependable child care during your absence. Pets will require care by a neighbor, relative, or dependable pet care facility. Regardless of your child care or pet care needs, plan ahead; it is another conference cost you will incur. Peace of mind knowing your children and pets are being well cared for means a more successful conference for you.

Cell Phone

Cell phone plans are changing constantly, and free nationwide calling is pretty common. The only cost is the air-time charges. Even if this is true in your area of coverage, it may not apply in distant cities and countries (roaming). You may be subject to per-minute roaming charges. So, you want to ask your cell phone company if you will have roaming charges in the conference location. This may not be a significant cost, but it is certainly one to consider, as you will probably be calling your significant other at least once a day, if he or she is not traveling with you. A checklist of possible indirect costs is provided in Table 3.2.

Travel Costs of Your Significant Other

Most conferences are held in interesting places, and there is a high probability that your significant other would also want to go to the conference

TABLE 3.2
Checklist of Indirect Conference Costs

Lost wages	$_____
New clothes	$_____
Boarding of pets	$_____
Babysitting for children	$_____
Cell phone charges	$_____
Total	$_____

location—even without attending the conference with you. Yes, there are some exceptions—there may be some very uninteresting places for specialized conferences that need to have a tour of sewers associated with the conference or that are held in a mosquito-infested tent to satisfy part of their constituency. On the other hand, one person's paradise is another person's least desirable place to visit. There would be no conference costs for your significant other, and the hotel costs for double occupancy are often the same as single occupancy. So, it seems like travel and meals are the primary costs of bringing your significant other. The additional travel costs could be zero if you are driving to the conference.

There may be conference costs if you bring your spouse to some of the conference events, like the annual banquet and awards ceremony.

Conversely, what are the costs of your significant other not going with you? Will they want their own week off to go to *their* conference, will they go shopping or have a night out with the boys or girls? If you are on a tight budget, these are costs you might want to consider and discuss.

Opportunity Costs

The authors attempt to define opportunity cost by asking the question "What else could I be doing with the time I spend preparing and going to the conference?" Do not underestimate the time that it takes to write the paper, registering, getting a hotel booked, and going to a conference. Being away from work, school, and home could mean missing being with the family, taking a class, exercising, working longer at work, a Cub Scout meeting, or attending a child's recital. These are personal decisions that need to be evaluated.

Who Will Pay for the Conference?

You can address this question now that you have an idea of the costs for the conference. There are generally only two sources that will fund you to go to a conference. One is the institution for which you work or study. The second is you.

Funding By Your Institution

Your trip to the conference might get funded if you work for a company (e.g., nonprofit, for-profit, government, etc.) or in the education field (e.g., faculty, professor, staff, board member, supervisor, etc.). If your trip to the conference gets funded, congratulations. But remember that you are still on your own for the indirect and opportunity costs. The key to getting funded by your company is to tell your management why attending the conference would benefit the company. It is also important to get authorization well in advance. It would not hurt to start mentioning the conference at least six months in advance because most arrangements will have to be finalized two or three months before the conference. It would even be good to work *attending the ABC conference* into your annual goals and performance review. (Hey, it can't hurt to ask!) Generally, you should have a firm commitment from the people who approve travel to conferences (your management) *before* you submit an abstract. If your company does fund you, be prepared to share your publication and conference results with your peers and management upon your return.

Funding By You

You want to take a long, hard look at the conference if you will be funding your trip to the conference yourself. A typical conference can easily exceed $1,000, and it could approach $2,000 for a week-long conference in Hawaii. Even an in-town conference could cost $300 to $600 for registration. The conference may be tax deductible, but you need to talk to an accountant about the tax deductibility and meeting the minimum income requirements of this conference as a business or educational expense before you attend. Even if it is tax deductible, you will still have to come up with the cash for the items in Table 3.1.

SIDEBAR

Resume/CV

Don't forget to budget some much deserved time after the conference to update your resume with the new section called *Publications*.

Summary

In addition to implicitly agreeing to attend and present a paper, you will have to pay for the privilege of presenting your idea. At some point during the decision process to write a paper for a conference, you have to ask yourself two questions:

1. How much will this conference cost?

2. Who will pay for it?

You must consider direct conference costs such as transportation, airport parking costs, food, hotel, and registration. You also need to consider the not-so-direct costs such as your time away from work, what to do with pets and children, what clothes you may need to buy for the conference, and roaming charges on your cell phone. What are the costs of your significant other going with you? There are also opportunity costs to consider. In other words, "What else could I be doing with the time I spend preparing and going to the conference, such as being with the family, taking a class, exercising, working longer at work, or attending a child's recital?"

Funding for the conference will come from either your institution of yourself. If you are the funding source, you need to ask yourself if you really want to pay $300 to $1,500 to present and publish your paper.

Bibliography

Ferrazzi, Keith, and Tahl Raz. *Never Eat Alone and Other Secrets to Success, One Relationship at a Time.* New York: Crown, 2005.

Many factors weigh in when making decisions about publishing.
(iStockphoto.com)

4

Publishing Rates

The gold standard for publications at hiring and tenure time is the peer-reviewed article. (Bucholtz 2010)

Introduction

A published article in a prestigious peer-reviewed journal is always best, but many of those articles begin as a conference paper. Many people ask about the whys and wheres of publishing, but one of the most common and poorly researched questions that continue to arise is how often others publish and what is expected of you for promotion, tenure, recognition, branding, or simply to see your name in print. This chapter discusses publishing in academia and industry and summarizes adult learning for the readers of this book. The authors have found that many people who do not need to publish for work will go through periods of publication highs and lows, streaks and droughts, peaks and valleys. The peaks will see the author getting into the publishing mode, researching conferences, doing extensive literature reviews of their topics, and searching for interesting conference topics in interesting places—or if you are on a tight budget, you will be looking for local conferences. The valleys will be periods of meditation, developing ideas, jotting down ideas, spending quality time with family, and generally preparing for the next phase of going back into your publishing mode. The valleys tend to be filled with *life*—work, family, house repairs, and your other passions. Your ability to publish may be enhanced or diminished based on whether you are in academia or industry. This chapter discusses both academic and industrial publishing and concludes with a personal publication challenge to the readers of this book.

Peer-Reviewed Journals versus Conference Publishing

You know there is a big difference between an article that you read in the local newspaper and one that you read in a *National Geographic* magazine. The articles in the *National Geographic* magazine have had a lot more time spent on them, have better artwork, and have undergone a lot more review before being published. The *National Geographic* article is a higher quality article. The same is true for conferences and peer-reviewed journals. Conferences get research data published quickly but acceptance is often based on a 150-word abstract. A peer-reviewed article is reviewed in its entirety by several reviewers who are conversant on the subject, and it may be rejected or accepted with modifications. The academic community does not include conference presentations and published conference proceedings in the same category with peer-reviewed journal publications, and you should never combine them on your resume/CV.

Academic Publishing

It is important to publish in peer-reviewed journals. Journal articles often start as a conference paper. The authors of this book like to publish papers and like to attend conferences. This may be because they are vain and like to see their names in print, have low self-confidence, like to go to conferences, tend to overachieve, believe in the publish-or-perish theory, or are trying to share their knowledge with others in their fields. Our need to publish is probably a combination of all the above.

Statistics

The authors believe this book can help would-be authors brand themselves and learn to step into the publishing landscape where they may have never ventured. This is important because it has been shown for business faculty in nine public universities that "years of professional experience, the number of publications, and a PhD or other terminal degree had a positive impact on faculty salary" (Webster 1995, 730). Another article described a study of the peer-reviewed publication history of 3,000 natural sciences faculty at 133 colleges and universities and found

- significant discipline-based differences
- significant gender-based differences
- less populated disciplines have a higher publication rate than in the traditional disciplines
- men publish more frequently than women (except in neuroscience)
- publication rates averaged from 0.51 to 1.17 publications per faculty member per year
- publication productivity increases with rank (Research Corporation 2001, 1)

Similarly, Fish and Gibbons (1989, 97) found that PhD economists had significantly (p <.001) different average publication rates of 1.76 and 1.01 for men and women, respectively. Rubin and Powell (1987) found that assistant professors with social work doctorates publish an average of 1.64 and 0.37 papers per year for men and women, respectively; 0.78 and 0.86 for associate professors; and 0.68 and 0.41 for professors.

Lee (2000, 139–144) studied the longitudinal publication trends of *successful* (graduating with a published dissertation) PhD doctoral students for every 5 years from 1965 to 1995 in the fields of analytical chemistry,

---

SIDEBAR

Solo-Authoring

Lee's longitudinal study from 1965 to 1995 noted a trend away from solo-authored papers.

experimental psychology, and American literature. He researched whether doctoral students published during a 5-year period bracketing the publication of their dissertation—from 3 years before to 1 year after the year the dissertation was published. Over his 30-year study period, Lee found that 64 to 86 percent (chemistry), 45 to 59 percent (psychology), and 7 to 35 percent (literature) of the students had at least one publication. He also found that 63 percent of all doctoral students in his study published in 1995, up from 43 percent in 1965. The mean number of publications for published authors varies (by year and discipline) from a low of 1.0 (in 1975 by psychology students) to 5.7 (in 1995 by chemistry students). Lee also noted a trend away from solo-authored papers.

One of the requirements of dissertations is that the information be publishable. Several PhD-granting institutions now require that doctoral students publish their work.

Adult Learning

Malcolm Knowles's (1998) book about the adult learner described the motivation of an adult learner (andragogy) and that it is necessarily different than that for a child (pedagogy). The authors describe next a few reasons an adult would want to publish.

It is important to publish papers and books because the experience of meeting people at conferences can be career enhancing (or career producing), and discussing your research passion with someone who understands your passion can be very stimulating. You learn in a conference environment and from other participants about the projects they are doing, how they resolved a problem, or how they would approach the situation you face when your return to your work.

It is important to publish papers and books because writing proves you have the depth of experience to take your project or hypothesis or research through to completion. It demonstrates you have the experience, that you've taken a scientific or scholarly approach to an issue, and have thoroughly thought it through. Being able to talk about a subject (in the presentation) is proof you've learned the subject to the point where others are willing to listen to you as a peer in your field.

SIDEBAR

Will Publishing Affect My Salary?

You would expect that publishing would be positively correlated with salary increases. Many journal articles get their start
as an article at a conference. They are refined, corrected, and
redirected based on feedback from the discussant and the conference attendees. Hilmer and Hilmer (2005, 516–517) surveyed
agricultural economists in academia and found "that the number of years since a faculty member received his or her PhD
is the most significant factor in determining his or her current
salary. ... [They further found] statistically significant economic
returns to articles published in top agricultural, regional agricultural, and the top 36 economic journals. Hence, the results
seem to confirm our prediction that agricultural economics de-
partments more highly reward articles published in top journals.
Among these journal types, each additional article published in a
regional agricultural economics journal increases annual salary by
1 percent, each additional article published in a top 36 economics journal increases annual salary by 0.8 percent, and each additional article published in a top agricultural economics journal
increases annual salary by 0.5 percent. It is somewhat surprising
that the returns from a regional agricultural economic journal
are twice that of a top agricultural economics journal, although
the difference is not statistically significant. This finding seems to
confirm Beilock and Polopolus's statement regarding the importance of regional agricultural economics journals for agricultural
economists. Note that the estimated effects of journal publications are roughly one-half or less of the estimated effect of each
additional year since PhD receipt. Nonetheless, it appears that
the agricultural economics market does provide financial incen-
tives for producing higher quality journal articles" (Hilmer and
Hilmer 2005, 516–517).

It is also important to publish papers and books because they are inherently self-directing. Authors can decide to write or not to write an article for a conference or a journal. Authors have total control over describing the topic and over the depth of discussion. In addition, it brands you in a specific area as an expert. As authors age and continue publishing scholarly works, their individual brand is reinforced.

Publishing helps you create a brand, develop contacts, and will probably increase your salary. Presenting and interacting with your peers at conferences helps you learn experientially. Describing the research you have done and the problems you have solved is an opportunity to share your knowledge and experience with your peers, faculty, and industry experts.

Publishing in Industry

There are many advantages to working outside of academia. There may be more funds for research and development, funding for new products, and you end up with goods (a real working widget) or a service as an end product. People are always interested in goods and services and how they were developed and produced. The one caution that needs to be stated is that your published paper should not be a blatant marketing effort or a sales brochure. Don't just make your paper a data sheet, or a syllabus, or an annual report from your company or class.

Unemployed

You can be unemployed for several reasons (e.g., layoff, being fired, graduate school, retired, family leave, etc.), and writing a paper for a conference is one of the best ways to make it back into the land of receiving a regular paycheck. Conferences are an excellent place to learn the latest trends and make contacts with key people in your industry.

Caution

Your published paper should not be a blatant marketing effort or a sales brochure.

Company Proprietary, Patents, and ITAR

There are also many restrictions to publishing if you are working in industry, government, or academia. These might include company proprietary topics, ideas that are in the process of being patented, and international traffic in arms regulations (ITAR) restrictions. Each of these topics is discussed in more detail in this section.

Examples of company proprietary topics are trade secrets, processes, formulas, software programs, drawings, schematics, and failure analyses. You can see that this category can include almost anything your company does because it can be used by another company without the effort (i.e., cost) that your company put into developing your goods or services. You will need to get approval from your company to publish anything that happened or was created in your company—even if you were the inventor. New employees generally sign an employee agreement stating that anything developed on company time is the property of the company. Don't get offended. They paid you to develop it; it's theirs; get their permission to publish it.

Ideas that are in the process of being patented may be the same items listed in the previous paragraph but have the possibility of being released to the public (e.g., a new color or design) that must be patented in order for the company to have sole ownership for the duration of the patent. You may be able to publish this information, but you'll have to identify it as "patent pending" or use other words that your legal department instructs you to use in your publication.

The international traffic in arms regulations (ITAR) restrictions were implemented under Section 38 of the Arms Export Control Act to control the export of defense articles and defense services from the Unites States. Items defined as defense articles and defense services are regulated exclusively by the Department of State and may not be exported. This includes the obvious exporting by physical movement out of the country by truck, ship, or plane. It also includes information that can be exported by mailing it in an overnight mail pouch, with a simple click of a mouse, or by publishing it in a conference in the United States. Yes, publishing! Publishing places the information in the public domain, and it can be viewed by anyone. It is not hard to imagine a group of people at your competitor

---

SIDEBAR

Ideas Developed on Company Time

Don't get offended. They paid you to develop it; it's theirs; get their permission to publish it.

---

in another country doing a daily search for your company's name or looking at every published article for pieces of information they could use. This is why you and your legal department need to be aware of ITAR regulations.

The purpose of this section was to scare you into doing the right thing. If you are thinking about publishing an article, get permission from your company before you even submit the abstract. Yes, even the abstract needs to be approved by many companies. Your abstract is a mini-summary of your paper; it may be disclosing company proprietary or patentable information; or it may be subject to ITAR export restrictions—or all three. Once you know that you can publish your idea, then it's time to step up to the challenge.

Personal Challenge

The authors have shown in earlier chapters that publishing is beneficial, if not absolutely required, for your career. An added benefit is that the world is generally interested in what you are studying. An earlier section in this chapter has shown that doctoral students published at the rate of one or two papers per year. The publication rate, for students that published, ranged from a low of 0.51 per year (Research Corporation 2001) to a high of 5.7 per year (Lee 2000, 142–143). Some of these were conference papers, some appeared in peer-reviewed journals, and some were a combination of both.

If you have an interesting topic, a new slant on a topic, or have the same slant but on a different demographic, then you have the basis for a published paper. The authors would like to challenge the reader (yes, that's you), especially those in a master's or doctoral program or those taking a writing class. The challenge is not necessarily to convince you that you want to publish (that's why you are reading this book) but how much to publish. If you are producing a master's thesis or a doctoral dissertation, then you and your fellow students or recent graduates should strive to attain the publishing rates in Table 4.1. Clapham (2005, 390) believes it is a scientific crime to not publish because your research might be irreproducible and would be lost. An example of this would be research about the public opinion on a terrorist attack inside the United States prior to September 11, 2001—that research can never be done again because events have affected the public's perceptions of terrorism in the United States. Several universities are aligned with this personal challenge and are incorporating a publishing requirement for doctoral students. There are three categories of publishing for most people.

The first category (*I want one publication*) is for most people. There will be a few that do not want to publish their work, do not have time, do not have the inclination, are prevented from publishing by their Institutional Review Board (IRB) or their company, or feel their work is not worthy of publication. However, most people are able to publish one paper based on their thesis or dissertation. You did some good work, and you should share that information with your peers. Your advisor probably likes to get published, and she may have added significantly to the development of your ideas and your writing. Writing a paper with your advisor and having her name on it is also good public relations. Their input will probably make it a better paper, and it might even get you accepted more easily at certain conferences. Your advisor is the one who will probably be called when you apply for a job or a teaching position, so it is always a good idea

TABLE 4.1
Publishing Rate Goals for Students in a Master's or Doctoral Program

Publication Style	Percentage of Class	Publishing Rate Goal
I want one publication	90%	I published paper during their studies
I like doing this	50%	I published paper per year
I'm a high achiever	10%	5 published papers per year

> **Hint**
>
> It is a good idea to keep your thesis advisor/dissertation chair involved with your publications.
>
> **Counter-Hint**
>
> If your advisor did not significantly contribute to the idea or analysis, or contribute something new to the paper, then your advisor should not be a co-author.

to keep your thesis advisor and dissertation chair involved with your publications. Another view of publishing with your advisor is accountability. If your advisor did not significantly contribute to the idea or analysis, or contribute something new to the paper, then your advisor should not be a co-author. This is sometimes a fine line of distinction and the reader is referred to the article by Costa and Gatz (1992, 4) for six scenarios of student-faculty collaboration.

The second category (*I like doing this*) includes the person that occasionally has a good publishable idea, may be selective in which conferences they publish, or only chooses to attend local conferences due to family or budget constraints. You may choose to publish at a specialized conference that is held only once a year. This will give you the opportunity to visit with peers, and there is a high likelihood that peers will be there every year or two since that is the only major conference discussing this specific topic.

Then there are the *high achievers* in the third category. You should aspire to be publishing five papers per year in high-quality journals if you plan to be in a tenure-track academic position. You should verify that publications are important to the institutions that you apply to—for example, many universities are considered teaching universities and may not value publications as much as research universities. Keep in mind that publishing rate is not the entire story; your field does not want you recycling the same paper over and over—this is considered plagiarism; even if you are copying from yourself. It is also very important that all of your

> **SIDEBAR**
>
> **How Many Should I Publish?**
>
> Hilmer and Hilmer (2005, 515) surveyed agricultural economists in academia and found "current faculty members in our sample have published an average of 15.52 peer-reviewed articles and 193.11 pages during their careers. The clear plurality of these articles, 5.58 or 36 percent, were published in top agricultural economics journals, with other economic and other agricultural economic journals comprising 22 percent and 20 percent, respectively. Finally, regional agriculture and top 36 economics journals bring up the rear with both comprising roughly 12 percent of total peer-reviewed publications" (Hilmer and Hilmer 2005, 515).

conference publications are scholarly. You don't want to develop a brand as a writer of poorly researched, poorly written, or recycled conference papers. The subject of plagiarism, ethics, and scholarly writing is important, and they are discussed in more detail in Chapters 9 and 11.

Ethical Dilemma—Publishing Using the Same Topic

What would happen if you used a paragraph or an entire section from one of your previously published articles in a future article? This could be considered a form of plagiarism and is an ethical issue. Yes, you can plagiarize yourself. You need to be publishing significantly new information in each paper. Writing several papers on a single broad topic is acceptable; that is how you show your depth of knowledge on a topic. However, you will want to make significant changes to the paper. For example, you might publish two papers on a similar topic but approach it from a human resource perspective once and either the finance or leadership aspect another time; or address the issues with the electrical circuit in one paper and

> **50 Percent Rule**
>
> Ethically, text, content, and artwork must change at least 50 percent in order to qualify as a new paper.

the thermodynamics or manufacturing issues in another paper; or write a paper reporting on a survey of union employees and then address the perspective of management or the effect on the local society in an alternate paper. There is no rule-of-thumb for how different one of your papers has to be from a previously published paper. The authors have used the 50 Percent Rule when modifying papers for a second conference: Text, content, or artwork must change at least 50 percent in order to qualify as a new paper. See the example of publishing several aspects of a research topic in Chapter 8.

Summary

Students who want to excel in industry or go into academia should publish at the rate of at least one peer-reviewed journal article per year to keep up with published averages. This will brand you for entry into industry, will increase your chances of being accepted into academic positions, and will help you command a higher salary.

Bibliography

Bucholtz, Mary. "Tips for Academic Publishing," http://www.linguistics.ucsb.edu/faculty/bucholtz/sociocultural/publishingtips.html (cited August 1, 2010).

Clapham, Phil. "Publish or Perish." *Bioscience* 55 (5) (2005): 390–391.

Costa, Martin, and Margaret Gatz. "Determination of Authorship Credit in Published Dissertations." *Psychological Science* 3 (6) (1992): 4.

Fish, Mary, and Jean D. Gibbons. "A Comparison of the Publications of Male and Female Economists." *Journal of Economic Education* 20 (1) (1989): 93–105.

Hilmer, Cristiana E., and Michael J. Hilmer. "How Do Journal Quality, Co-Authorship, and Author Order Affect Agricultural Economists' Salaries?" *American Journal of Agricultural Economics* 87 (2) (2005): 509–523.

Knowles, Malcolm S., Elwood F. Holton III, and Richard A. Swanson. *The Adult Learner: The Definitive Classic in Adult Education and Human Resource Development.* 5th edition. Houston, TX: Gulf Professional Publishing, 1998.

Lee, Wade M. "Publication Trends of Doctoral Students in Three Fields, from 1965–1995." *Journal of the American Society for Information Science* 51 (2) (2000): 139–144.

Research Corporation. *Determining Publication Productivity and Grant Activity among Science Faculty at Surveyed Institutions.* Tucson: Research Corporation, 2001.

Rubin, Allen, and David Powell. "Gender and Publication Rates: A Reassessment with Population Data." *Social Work* (1987): 317–320.

Webster, Allen L. "Demographic Factors Affecting Faculty Salary." *Educational and Psychological Measurement* 55 (5) (1995): 726–735.

Section II

Finding the Right Conference

The chapters in the previous section identified some of the reasons why you might want to publish at a conference and how to budget expected costs. This section walks you through the next phases of your journey into the publishing landscape.

5. How Do I Find Out About Conferences?

6. What Do I Look for in a Call for Papers?

7. The Timeline for Conference Papers

The first step in writing a conference paper is finding the conferences that might interest you. You will usually find the necessary information from an announcement called a *call for papers* or a *call for proposals,* and Chapter 5 describes how to find these announcements. The next step (Chapter 6) discusses the analysis process to quickly extract the needed information from a call for papers. This will allow you to promptly review a dozen calls and see if there is one that is a good match for your idea. The final chapter in this section (Chapter 7) discusses the timeline that is needed to produce a quality paper within the time constraints typically imposed by a conference planning committee. Different conferences have different submission criteria and dates, but you will need to identify a conference and write a paper within a few short months. A special section has been added to caution the future conference-paper writer about the quality of conferences. Let's get started by finding a conference.

Location is an important part of conferences, and calls for conference presentations can come from all over the world. (iStockphoto.com)

5

Finding Conferences

The Internet is a wonderful place to find calls for papers.

Introduction

Now that you know that you want to be published, how do you go about finding a suitable conference? There are two ways. One is to look around you and use the resources immediately available to you such as professional magazines that you subscribe to, advice from other people in your field, coworkers, classroom professor, program directors, or the dean. The second way to find out about conferences is a more generic search of the Internet. This chapter provides many different suggestions to help you find an appropriate conference, and the authors conclude with a discussion about the quality of conferences. Some conferences are lower quality and have a high acceptance rate; others are at the top of the conference food chain and have acceptance rates as low as 20 percent. Let's start with the easiest way to find a conference and then expand your search to the World Wide Web.

Look Around You

There are conferences on almost every subject, including business, education, engineering, physics, history, literature, collectibles, nursing, medicine, banking, escrow, and the unimaginable. The first place to look is right where you are. You probably have some professional journals or trade magazines on your desk at work, on your desk at home, next to the easy chair in the living room, on your coffee table, in the back seat of the car, and there might even be one in your mailbox. You probably have one in your briefcase that you have been hauling between home and work for two weeks, thinking that you will eventually read it. There is a high probability that you don't even have to move. Look around you, pick it up now, and look at it.

Magazines

The authors don't mean the magazines that you get at the grocery store. These are the magazines that you receive as a professional. They might come from your professional society, or they may be industry trade publications that are distributed free to qualified individuals. There is often a section in the president's or editor's section telling you that a conference is coming and to plan for it. There might be an announcement and a call for papers if it is the right time of the year (usually about six months before the conference), or there will be an article on last year's conference. Don't ignore these. There are two advantages to these after-conference critiques. If the conference date has passed this year, you can start planning for next year. The other advantage is being able to see pictures from the conference. It gives you a sense of the size of the sessions, the type of people who attend, and the dress code for this type of conference. Dress codes will be discussed in Chapter 12.

Journals

Many peer-reviewed journal articles start out as an idea that was presented at a conference. If there is a journal on a subject, there is probably at least one conference dedicated to the subject. If the conference and journal are related (i.e., produced by the same sponsoring professional society), the journal will occasionally publish a call for papers. It is usually found in the back three to five pages of the journal.

Newsletters

Professional societies or any special interest group will usually have a newsletter. It may be published on paper or online, and it is a very good source for conference information. The newsletter will have information on the conference and will usually lead you to a Web site that you can check out for more information. Newsletters are also more likely to have an article about last year's conference with pictures of the winners at the awards ceremony, as well as the luncheon, the banquet, the exhibitor booths, or the keynote address presenter.

You might actually have to get up once you have exhausted the magazines, journals and newsletters around you. At the very least, you will have to reach for a computer and send an e-mail to one of your professors or a coworker.

Professors

The saying *publish or perish* is often used to refer to assistant professors who have not yet achieved tenure. There is a desire in academic circles to publish scholarly peer-reviewed articles and books to show progress and growth. So you might ask some of your professors about upcoming conferences, conferences where they have published in the past, and any interesting calls for papers that may have crossed their desks. They may even be interested in co-authoring a paper with you. Some professors are not interested in publishing and may not have any suggestions, or your topic of interest may not mesh with the conferences they suggest. However, you will learn about other conferences, and you may have a paper to submit for that conference in a future year.

Coworkers

Publishing is less of a requirement outside of academic circles, but there is still a large body of people in industry who volunteer to work in professional organizations. They work on finance committees, membership drives, review papers, organize conferences, and some of them are still on the cutting edge of their field and are known to publish papers. Your coworkers may not be the ones publishing, but they may know those who are publishing or know of upcoming conferences. Ask around.

Look at the bulletin boards or electronic message boards at work or at school. People post the most interesting items on bulletin boards, and there may even be a call for papers up there. Once you have exhausted the human and paper sources for conferences, it's time to look online.

Look Online

If you didn't find a topic of interest for publishing in any magazines, journals, or newsletters, or your coworkers and professors are unable to suggest conferences for you at this time, the Internet is another almost bottomless resource.

Known Web Sites

The Internet is a wonderful place to find things, but the authors have found that not all conferences are listed. The authors wanted to find a certain Web site, performed a search with several search engines, and came up with no hits. Sometimes you need to have someone tell you where to look or have them send you the Web address for a specific conference. Some popular conferences are listed in Chapter 6.

Search Engines

You may not be able to find a particular conference that you know exists. However, you might type too few words into a search engine and have 162,437 entries returned to you. The authors do not have a magic recipe, but you might want to go to your favorite search engine and put in the following search words.

- *"Call for paper"* or *"call for proposal."* The authors recommend adding the quotes around the term *call for papers*. However, search engines have gotten more sophisticated and it may no longer be necessary for most search engines.
- *Conference.* This is an important word to distinguish the call for papers from a magazine, or journal, or an online publishing site.
- *Leadership.* It is important to list your topic(s) of interests to help eliminate the conferences that do not apply to your field of interest. You may embellish this bullet by adding other topics like "educational" if you want to publish in the field of *educational leadership.*

You may want to put some of these words in quotes if you have a specific type of conference in mind (e.g., *"educational conference"* or *"business conference"*).

- *2012.* You can insert any year in which you want to present your paper. Otherwise, you may get calls for papers from 1998. A refinement of the year search term is to add the month of the conference if you have identified a specific month for travel.

- *Hawaii.* Identifying the location by city, state, or country can help reduce the breadth of the search results. This is particularly useful if you want to present your paper locally to minimize travel costs, or if you have a particular destination in mind. Some people try to schedule a vacation around a conference. It might be difficult to find a conference on *Caribbean Economic Conditions* in Paris, France, in August, but you might be able to find a conference if your dates are flexible and if your vacation plans include popular conference locations such as Boston, Las Vegas, Los Angeles, Miami, Orlando, San Diego, San Francisco, Toronto, Vancouver, or Washington, D.C.

The preceding terms might look like Figure 5.1 on your screen. A search of this particular string of words, on a popular search engine, yielded 82 hits at one point during the writing of this book. Adding January to the search criteria yielded 27 hits; this made the review and downselection much easier.

You may want to try different search engines because they are not all the same. The specific set of words shown in Figure 5.1 ("call for paper" conference leadership educational 2012) were used in several search engines, and the results are listed in Table 5.1. This does not imply that the search engine with the most hits is the best, because you might get a lot of garbage and may have to spend too much time sifting through a hundred

---

"call for paper" conference leadership educational 2012

Figure 5.1.
Search Screen for Example in the Text

TABLE 5.1
Results from Various Search Engines, in Alphabetical Order, for the Following Sequence of Words: "call for paper" conference leadership educational 2012

Search Engine Used	Number of Hits
http://www.altavista.com/	490
http://search.aol.com/aol/	269
http://www.ask.com/	1,050
http://www.dogpile.com/	58
http://www.excite.com/	651
http://www.gigablast.com/	13
http://www.google.com	872
http://iwon.ask.com/	151
http://www.joeant.com/	1,606
http://www.lycos.com	364
http://search.msn.com/	8,830
http://www.bing.com/	872
http://www.webcrawler.com/	48
http://www.yahoo.com	1,990

or more hits. However, the other extreme (zero hits) is not good either! Examples of search results are presented in Table 5.1.

These searches will change with time as some Web sites are added and deleted. The authors have included two calls for papers in the appendices of Chapter 6.

Searching the Internet for calls for papers can be quite entertaining. You will find conferences in interesting places, in boring places, around the corner from you, and in places that you've never heard of. You will find conferences that you never imagined would attract people, and professionally designed Web sites for conferences that will have less than 30 people in attendance. You will find Web sites that are incomplete in that they omit seemingly important information like the due date of the abstract, where to send the abstract, who to send the registration to, and whether or not the papers will be published or simply presented. You will also find Web sites that have nothing to do with what you want. There will be several calls for papers from previous years, and there will be Web sites in languages other than your own.

Now that you know about finding conferences, you might ask yourself if all conferences are created equal. The answer is no, and conference quality is described in the next section.

Are There Different Levels of Quality of Conferences?

Before you dive into publishing, you should ask yourself about the quality of the conference. Yes, there are different quality levels of conferences in addition to specialized conferences, regional conferences, topical conferences, and company conferences. This is not discussed very much, but the authors wanted to point this out to the reader. For example, there are quality levels for many other forms of expression. There is a difference between publishing a letter in your homeowner association newsletter and in the *Harvard Business Review*, just as there is a difference between publishing a picture in a Betty Boop collectibles magazine and one in *National Geographic*. Gardening in your yard may have a different level of quality than in the White House Rose Garden.

The authors have defined a set of conference quality levels and listed the definitions of these different levels. The authors judiciously picked M (an abbreviation for Mallette Conference Quality Level) and the numbers zero through three. This discussion will start with the conference types that have the easiest acceptance criteria (M0) and progress through to the more scholarly conferences (M3). Your ultimate goal should be to publish and present at the best (highest quality) conference possible and to eventually turn your idea into a peer-reviewed journal article.

Conference Quality

Your ultimate goal should be to publish and present at the best (highest quality) conference possible and to eventually turn your idea into a journal article.

Level M-Zero (M0) Conferences

If you *really* want to get published, there are conferences that will accept your abstract and paper with very little review. The major requirement is that you pay the conference registration fees. In some cases, you don't even have to show up to present the paper (although the authors strongly discourage this practice); it will be published if you pay the registration fee. The registration fee is often quite high, sometimes twice the cost of other conferences. The authors suspect that the conference organizing committee members are subsidized for their registration, travel, hotel, and/or meals by your registration fee. The abstract acceptance rate at these conferences often approaches 100 percent, so you have a very good chance of getting your abstract accepted. This is not to say that M0 level conferences have no standards; it simply implies that their standards are lower and that they accept weaker abstracts. These conferences should not be ignored, as they are a good place to start your publishing career and network with other people who also *really* want to get published. Many major conferences started as small regional conclaves and have grown to be premier international conferences. On the plus side, M0 level conferences are often held in very appealing locations (such as Cancun, Mexico) and can be very entertaining (maybe even educational) due to the diverse range of topics that were accepted and are presented.

There is a trend toward publishing on the Web, and the reader may want to follow the discussions of *open access* (OA) journals. However, anyone can create a Web site and paste an article in there. These articles may be quite scholarly (see Chapter 11) but may not have been peer reviewed and may be bogus. Conferences that only publish their papers on a Web site may fall into the M0 level.

It may be difficult to identify M0 level conferences. A ritzy location is not a positive sign of an M0 level conference. High quality conferences are also held in popular destination cities, overseas, and at ski resorts. However, you might want to do a little further checking if the conference is being held on a cruise ship! Registration fees sometimes do not tell the whole story either. There may be some subtle costs that are covered by registration—like the inclusion of meals, entertainment at the banquet, a stipend for the keynote presenter, transportation and a tour of a nearby facility, the unusually high cost of the conference meeting rooms at the hotel, or simply a tendency of your professional society to offset other costs of the organization. Conference attendance is also not a good indicator. There are some professions where the number of experts in a specialized discipline may comprise only a few dozen participants.

Level M1 Conferences

M1 level conferences accept papers based on a thorough review of the abstract only. The vast majority of conferences fall into this category. The program directors do not have the resources (which are usually voluntary) to review full papers in detail. Lack of peer review is the primary reason that conference papers are not generally considered primary publication, even if all other requirements (such as first time published, broadly disseminated, retrievable, methods explained, and duplicable) are satisfied. Almost every conference falls into this category.

Level M2 Conferences

M2 level conferences usually have a two-stage approach to accepting papers. The first step is accepting the abstract—this is identical to the level M1 conferences described above. The second step is a submittal and review of the full paper *prior* to the conference. These preliminary papers are reviewed in their entirety and are not subjected to a blind review (see sidebar). Papers for the conference are either (1) accepted, (2) accepted with comments, or (3) rejected based on full paper review.

Papers that are accepted or accepted with comments must be resubmitted in publication-ready (what used to be called camera-ready) format at a specific time before the conference—usually about a month or two before the conference. An example of a conference that uses this type of review process is the Institute of Electrical and Electronics Engineers (IEEE) Aerospace Conference (www.aero.org).

Level M3 Conferences

M3 level conferences differ from M2 level conferences in that they will accept your paper based on a blind peer review. M2 level conferences do

---

SIDEBAR

What Is a Blind Review?

A blind review is a method that is used to eliminate positive or negative personal bias toward an author or institution when evaluating a paper. All references to the author(s) and their institution(s) are deleted from the abstract or paper before review. This helps to equalize the process, especially if the field is filled with politics, is dominated by one company or university, there are graybeards (older experts) who are allowed to continue publishing only for their name, or when students are allowed to submit less scholarly papers. A blind review allows the paper to be evaluated solely on its own merits and not be influenced by personal or personnel biases.

---

not use a blind review process. The review might be done on a full copy of the paper or a summary. For example, the American Educational Research Association (AERA) Annual Conference requires a 2,000-word summary be submitted with the abstract for their blind review process. These summaries are reviewed in their entirety. Papers are either (1) accepted, (2) accepted with comments, or (3) rejected, based on the 2,000-word summary review. The AERA annual conference has rejection rates above 70 percent. Bucholtz (2010, 1) tells us that a blind review "can be a bit unpleasant: people are often very frank, and sometimes blunt."

Summary

This chapter highlighted some of the ways in which you could find a suitable conference and call for papers for your topic. Many of the sources are probably within reach of where you are sitting, and some of the suggested sources were literature (magazines, journals, and newsletters), people (friends, professors, and coworkers), and a search of online sources. Another part of evaluating a conference for suitability is determining conference quality. Researchers who are new to conference publishing should be aware that conferences have differing quality levels, from the easiest abstract acceptance criteria (M0) progressing through to the more scholarly conferences (M3) with their high abstract rejection rates.

Bibliography

Bucholtz, Mary. "Tips for Academic Publishing," http://www.linguistics. ucsb.edu/faculty/bucholtz/sociocultural/publishingtips.html (cited August 1, 2010).

One of the important aspects of selecting calls for papers is determining which conferences mesh with your own schedule demands. (iStockphoto.com)

6

Dissecting the Call for Papers

Conferences are very often held in intriguing and appealing places.

Introduction

Most people hear about a conference and consider submitting a paper based on finding (Chapter 5) and reviewing a *call for papers* (this chapter). As mentioned in Chapter 5, such calls go by various names; for example, a call for papers is sometimes referred to as a *call for proposals*. This call will be your introduction to the conference and includes most of the information that you will need. There are six steps to evaluating a call for papers.

Step 1.   Look at the conference title and ask yourself: "Is it in my field?"

Step 2.   Look at the abstract due date and ask yourself: "Is it in the future?"

Step 3.   Look at where and when it will be held and ask yourself: "Do I want to go?"

Step 4.   Ask yourself: "Who will pay for it?"

Step 5.   Look at the conference theme and topics and ask yourself: "Does it help my brand?"

Step 6.   Ask yourself: "What steps do I have to take?"

Steps 1 through 6 are discussed in more detail in this chapter. The process of evaluating a call for papers could take you days of contemplation, but it should only take a few seconds for the first five steps and a few minutes for a basic evaluation of the last step.

What Do the Calls for Papers Have in Common?

All calls for papers have a few common items in the first few lines. These include the title of the conference, the location, and the date(s) of the conference. The hotel, school, or convention center where the conference will be held may be included somewhere in the body of the call. The next few lines will discuss the theme of the conference and may include several topic area suggestions. Examples are shown in Appendices 6A and 6B.

The remainder of the call will discuss submission guidelines. This section of the call will always include the due date of the abstract or summary or paper, and it will also include the information about how to submit the abstract. See Table 6.1 for details of what can be found in a call for papers. The current trend is to submit your abstract online; most conferences discourage paper submittals and many will not even accept paper submittals. The call for papers may include a required minimum or maximum word count, a specific format, and may ask you to include your affiliation.

TABLE 6.1
What Do Calls for Papers Have in Common?

Calls for Papers *Will* Include	Calls for Papers *May* Include
Name of conference	Theme and topics for sessions
Location/city	Hotel information
Date(s) of conference	Map to the hotel or conference location
Due date of abstract	Featured or keynote presenter(s)
Submittal instructions	Abstract-formatting information: word count, columns, font size, attachment file type, blind-review instructions
	City and side trip information
	Spouse's program, lunches, banquets, dress code

This section prepared you for what to expect in the call for papers. The next section will take you through the thought process to eliminate conferences that won't work for you and to find the best conference for your paper. So, you want to ask, "Is this conference for me?"

Is This Conference for Me?

The authors often refer to the first three steps as the environmental steps because they identify a subset of the publication landscape—they narrow down the time, the location, and the field of study. So the first thing to do when looking at a call for papers is to look at the title.

Step 1. Is It in My Field?

The conference title will tell you most of what you want to know about the conference. Ask yourself if it is in your field. The title may be quite broad (International Conference on Business), and it is likely that you could mold your paper idea into a possible topic. The title might be quite specific (8th International Conference on Global Spatial Data Infrastructure, or Psychometric Variables of Vietnamese Unwed Mothers), and you will promptly ignore it unless you are working on an interesting aspect of GPS tracking stations or with unwed mothers. Once you have bonded a bit with the title (this should take about 15 seconds), the next step is to look at the due date.

Step 2. Is It in the Future?

You have a chance to prepare and submit an abstract if the due date is in the future. Good. This took another 10 seconds. See the sidebar Submittals beyond the Due Date if you are past the due date. The final environmental step is to find the location and date of the conference.

Step 3. Do I Want to Go?

Conferences are very often held in intriguing and appealing places, and you might be interested in visiting the city, state, or country that is hosting the conference. Some conferences are held in places such as Hawaii—a

---

SIDEBAR

Submittals beyond the Due Date

Dates are dates. You don't want to be late for some dates (like your wedding). However, the abstract due date was created by someone who wanted to have the abstracts by a certain weekend to sort through them and get them dispatched to the reviewers in a timely fashion. This person may be like you and may have given themselves a few days or a week to do the work. Maybe they even expect a normal bell-shaped distribution of submittals based on the archaic abstract submittals via the postal system— not knowing what day a specific letter might be received. If you really have a topic that is germane to the conference, and you can submit it a week or two late; then shoot off an e-mail to the program director stating your topic, how well it would fit into their conference, and *humbly* ask permission to accept the submission of the late abstract. The paper review committee chairman may reject it, or they may find that it fits nicely into a four-paper session that only had two or three abstracts submitted. You can't lose by trying! The authors recommend that you think about the program chairperson's already overworked schedule— acknowledge the late submittal and respectfully request that the program chairperson consider your submission. You may even want to help by briefly suggesting your paper would be ideal for a particular session or topic. Be tactful, be brief, be humble, be professional, and be polite with all your submissions, especially your late submissions.

---

state that is not accessible by car for all but a lucky few people. Other conferences are held in Orlando, Florida, or in the huge convention center in Anaheim, California. Coincidentally, these locations are very near some very large amusement parks. Many people find Las Vegas fascinating and there are many large conference facilities in this town. Because of this, there are a large number of conferences and conventions held there every week of the year. Palm Springs (and the entire Coachella Valley) has hundreds of golf courses, and the average daily temperature in February is 75 degrees when much of the country is below freezing. In fact, most places in the world have something to offer to a group of people. Many people look for conferences in ski areas during the winter (see Appendix 6A), whereas others look for conferences in warm climates during the winter (see Appendix 6B). Other people look for local conferences to keep travel costs down or to minimize time away from work or family. Various conferences will appeal to your different (professional as well as personal) interests. You can probably find several good conference choices that appeal to you in these first three steps. Then it is time to think about the costs in the next step.

Step 4. Who Will Pay for It?

The first part of this process is to understand the costs. Costs are discussed in greater detail in Chapter 3. For a preliminary estimate of costs, you have to consider direct conference costs such as transportation, parking costs at the airport, food, hotel, and conference registration. There are also the not-so-direct costs to consider, like your time away from work or the costs of your significant other going with you (after all, most conferences are held in places where they might want to visit). There are also opportunity costs to consider (what else could I be doing with the time I will spend preparing and going to the conference?).

Once you have determined the approximate costs, it's time to determine who will pay for the direct costs. There is a possibility of being funded by your company or university if you are fortunate enough to be employed. In addition, some universities have a small fund to partially cover conference expenses for graduate students or your research project may have a budget for conference trips. Congratulations to those of you who can get some conference expenses covered, but you are still on your own for the indirect and opportunity costs. The key to getting funded by your company is to get authorization well in advance—maybe even suggest it in this year's performance goals with your manager. It would not hurt to start mentioning the conference at least six months in advance because most arrangements will have to be finalized two or three months in advance. Generally, you should have a firm payment commitment from yourself or your employer *before* you submit an abstract.

You must attend the conference—the ethics of submitting a paper without intending to present it are discussed in Chapter 12, but canceling after your abstract is accepted is something you want to avoid. If you have to fund the entire cost of the conference, then you need to ask yourself if you really want to pay $300 to $1,500 (depending on conference duration and location) to publish your research.

Another issue to consider is the quality of the conference. Do you want to be accepted at a low-level conference or risk not being accepted at a premium top-of-the-food-chain conference? The section at the end of Chapter 5 discussed levels of conference *quality*. Once you get through the first four steps, you will have determined whether this is a possible conference for you. Then it's time to get serious about publishing.

Step 5. Does It Help My Brand?

The theme may give you a clue as to whether your subject of interest would be acceptable to the conference. There is often a list of topics that are applicable to the conference; these are often the titles of the sessions that will comprise the conference. Your abstract should fall into one of these categories and for review purposes, you may be asked to identify which session or track should review your abstract.

Some calls for papers have neither a theme nor a list of topics. In this case, use the general theme as depicted by the name of the conference. For example, the Annual Hemingway Conference would lead you to submit an

---

Question

You need to ask yourself if you really want to pay $300 to $1,500 to publish a paper.

Actual cost will vary depending on conference duration and location.

abstract that has a Hemingway-related topic. Clearly, you would not submit the earlier-mentioned GPS tracking station paper to this conference unless you are trying to get a rejection letter. Now you want to look for the specifics of submitting your abstract.

There are different formats for presentations at a conference. These include formal paper presentations, panel discussions, table discussions, poster sessions, and keynote addresses. These are individually discussed in Chapter 6. Finally, what do you have to do?

Step 6. What Steps Do I Have to Take?

The submission steps will depend on the type of participation. These participation styles can include the writing of a paper and the presenting of that paper in front of a group of your peers. It can also include poster sessions, panel discussions, table discussions, and keynote addresses. The steps required to submit your abstract are sometimes listed on another page or Web site, are vague, or are missing completely. If a format is prescribed, pay strict attention to those formatting guidelines. Abstracts have been rejected for incorrect formatting. People expect certain formats and will be distracted by your unusual style if you do not use the requested format. An example of the partial required submission criteria for contributors to American Educational Research Association (AERA) journals is given here.

> The preferred style guide for all AERA journals is the *Publication Manual of the American Psychological Association,* 5th ed., 2001.... *The Chicago Manual of Style,* 15th ed., 2003, is also acceptable for all AERA journals.
>
> Manuscripts should be typed on 8½ × 11-inch white paper, upper and lower case, double-spaced in entirety, with 1-inch margins on all sides. The type size should be at least 10 pitch (CPI) or 12 point. Subheads should be at reasonable intervals to break the monotony of lengthy text. Words to be set in italics (contrary to the rules of the style manual) should be set in italics, not underlined; sentence structure should be used to create emphasis. Abbreviations and acronyms should be spelled out at first mention unless they are found as entries

in their abbreviated form in *Merriam-Webster's Collegiate Dictionary,* 11th ed., 2003.

Pages should be numbered consecutively, beginning with the page after the title page. Mathematical symbols and Greek letters should be clearly marked to indicate italics, boldface, superscript, and subscript. [This section goes on to address requirements for computer discs, electronic submission, author identification, footnotes and references, tables, figures, illustrations, review process, originality of manuscript, copyright, comments, right of reply, and grievances.] (Editor 2005, 28–29)

The conference will occasionally publish an electronic template for the final paper submission. Use the final paper template, if one is provided, for the submission of your abstract. An example of a one-page formatting guideline from the Institute of Electrical and Electronics Engineers (IEEE) Aerospace Conference (Bryan 2004, 9) is shown in Table 6.2 and an example of an electronic template for papers can be found in the "author's info" section of that conference's Web site (http://www.aeroconf.org/).

TABLE 6.2

Paper and Size:
   Paper size/type .... White 8½" × 11"
   Number of pages 6–20
   (Or longer if required by the nature of the material. Invited papers are individually determined.)

Margins:
   Top and bottom margins .... 3/4"
   Left and right margins .... 3/4"

Columns:
   Number of columns 2
   Space between .... 1/4"

Title:
   Title typeface .... Bold 20 pt
   Times Roman upper and lower case, text centered on the full-page width. Initial caps on all words except articles. Keep less than 100 characters.

TABLE 6.2 (*continued*)

Author:

Typeface .... 10 pt
Times Roman upper and lower case, centered on the full-page width. Include affiliation, address, phone number, and e-mail. Do not include degrees or titles except military rank.

Text:

Typeface .... Times Roman 10 pt
Line-to-line spacing...single
Space after paragraph.. 10 pt
Paragraph indent .... None
Justification .... Left and right

Acronyms:

Define all acronyms on first usage.
Page numbers:...Bottom center of every page.

Footnotes:

Font size...8 point

Copyright Notice Footnote:

Include a copyright notice as a footnote on the first page: 0-7803-8870-4/05/$20.00
©2005 IEEE
Paper number Footnote: Put your paper number in a footnote on the first page.

Headings:

• Spacing before major or subheading ....Double space
• Spacing after major or subheading... 1½ space
• Major headings..Center, use 12 point SMALL CAPS, BOLD
• Subheadings Italic, flush left, separate line, same size as text
• Subsubheadings: Italic, run into paragraph with em dash

Equations:

• Where? .... Centered
• Equation numbers: In parentheses, flush with right side of column

Figure and Table Titles:

• Where? ....Directly below figure
• Where? ....Directly above table
• Font size? .... 10 point
• Scanned Image .... 300 dpi
• Image format...300 dpi JPEG

References:

• Where? .... End of paper
• Font..Times Roman 10 point

TABLE 6.2 (*continued*)

• References numbers.. In square brackets
• Style..As shown in examples

Biography:
    Include a brief biography and photo of each author.

Electronic copy:
    • Submit electronic copies both with the review copy and the final paper. No hard copy with final.
    • Remove passwords from paper.
    • Scan for viruses.

Document properties:
    Put your paper's title in Word "Properties" or in PDF "Document Properties."

The review manuscript (3 stapled copies) and filled-out IEEE copyright release form must be mailed to:

                _____, Paper Review Chair
                Conferences Office Address: xxx

If the format information is missing from the conference guidelines, the authors recommend submitting a 300- to 500-word abstract (not counting titles, names, affiliations, addresses, figures, photographs, or references). Use a format similar to the papers submitted at last year's conference—same author information at the top, same number of columns, single- or double-spaced text. Try to estimate the font size, and use right justification of paragraphs if that was done last year.

As a last resort, if you don't have a guide (like last year's conference digest), then submit a 300-word abstract using 12 point Times New Roman font, single column, double spaced, no right justification, and an indent at the beginning of each paragraph. An example, if no formatting guidelines are provided, is shown in Figure 6.1.

Summary

This chapter defined how to evaluate if a conference is appropriate for your topic of interest based on a discriminating review of a call for papers. The six steps that you must use when evaluating a call for papers are:

> *Abstract Submission for ABC Conference*
>
> Suggested Format if Formatting Guidelines Are Not Provided
>
> Dr. Leo Mallette
>
> Mallette Consulting, *[+ contact information]*
>
> Abstract
>
> Use 12 point Times New Roman style font, single column, double spaced, no right justification, and an indent at the beginning of each paragraph, . . . *and so on for about 300 to 500 words.*

Figure 6.1.
Authors' Suggested Format if Formatting Guidelines Are Not Provided
Source: G. Edward Bryan, "Author's Instructions for 2005 IEEE Aerospace Conference," http://www. aeroconf.org/2005_Web/05IEEE_InstructionsV7October27.doc (used with permission).

Step 1. Look at the conference title and ask yourself: "Is it in my field?"

Step 2. Look at the abstract due date and ask yourself: "Is it in the future?"

Step 3. Look at where and when it will be held and ask yourself: "Do I want to go?"

Step 4. Ask yourself: "Who will pay for it?"

Step 5. Look at the conference theme and topics and ask yourself: "Does it help my brand?"

Step 6. Ask yourself: "What steps do I have to take?"

Bibliography

Bryan, G. Edward. "Author's Instructions for 2005 IEEE Aerospace Conference," http://www.aeroconf.org/2005_Web/05IEEE_InstructionsV7 October27.doc (cited August 12, 2004).

Editor. "General Information for Contributors to AERA Journals." *Educational Researcher* 34 (2) (2005): 28–29.

Appendix 6A

Abbreviated Call for Papers for the 2006 IEEE Aerospace Conference (facing page)

Conference Web site: http://www.aeroconf.org

- Conference name is very clear, and the dates are obvious. Unless you are in the field, you might not know that IEEE and AIAA stand for the *Institute of Electrical and Electronics Engineers* and *American Institute of Aeronautics and Astronautics* respectively, in which case, you probably are not going to be submitting an abstract to this conference.

- The location is also obvious, but you might have to look up Big Sky, Montana, on Google Maps. Hmm, it looks like an interesting part of Montana in early March.

- The due dates are *very* obvious, but how do you submit the abstract? The reader is told that this should be done through the Web site.

- The Web site says this is the 27th annual conference, so you know this is not a fly-by-night conference, and the organizers have been doing it for a long time.

- It was mentioned in *Aviation Week.* That's a good recommendation.

- The specific areas of interest within aerospace are listed. This will give you a better indication that the conference is a good match for your paper. Very good.

- Several people are listed with e-mail and phone numbers. Good.

2011 IEEE Aerospace Conference
AIAA—Technical Cosponsor
March 5–12, 2011 Big Sky, Montana

Call for Papers

Abstract (300–500 words) due: July 1, 2010
Draft paper (6–20 pages) deadline: October 26, 2010
Reviewed paper returned to author: November 12, 2010
Final paper deadline: January 11, 2011
All submissions are electronic at: www.aeroconf.org

Technical Program

This Call invites submission of papers reporting original work or state-of-the-art reviews that enhance knowledge of: (1) aerospace systems, science, and technology; (2) applications of aerospace systems or technology to military, civil or commercial endeavors; (3) system engineering and management science in the aerospace industry; and (4) government policy that directs or drives aerospace programs, systems, and technologies. The technical program will present key innovations and achievements in aerospace technologies and their current and future applications.

14 Tracks

1. Eight Plenary Sessions: Science & Aerospace Frontiers (Key addresses by leading scientists and leaders in government and industry)
   (>100 Technical Sessions—See "Call for Papers" at www.aeroconf.org)

Junior Engineering and Science Conference

A concurrent conference for junior engineers, grades K–12
See "Junior Engineering" at www.aeroconf.org
More information: Website: www.aeroconf.org

Conference Chair:
David Woerner   david.woerner@jpl.nasa.gov   (818) 393-xxxx

Technical Program:
Richard Mattingly   richard.l.mattingly@jpl.nasa.gov   (818) 354-xxxx
Karen Profet   karen.profet@aeroconf.org   (310) 545-xxxx
Ed Bryan   edbryan@alumni.caltech.edu   (310) 454-xxxx
Mel Montemerlo   montemerlo@gmail.com   (703) 455-xxxx

Abstracts Chair:
Vahraz Jamnejad   vahraz.jamnejad@jpl.nasa.gov   (818) 354-xxxx

Registration:
Monica Panno   panica@earthlink.net   (818) 654-xxxx

Appendix 6B

Abbreviated Call for Papers for Hawaii International Conference on Education (facing page)

Web site: http://www.hiceducation.org/cfp_edu.htm

The authors have reformatted (a nice word for "deleted lots of stuff") the four-page-long call for papers to help familiarize you with call for papers at a glance. This conference call for papers is a good example of a widely popular conference in a desirable location.

- Conference name is very clear, and the dates are obvious.
- The location is also obvious; everyone knows about Honolulu.
- The submission deadline dates are *very* obvious; there are suggested topics, suggested formats for presentation, and they tell you how and where (Web site) to submit the abstract.
- The suggested topics cover all aspects of education and then some. It looks like a general conference, not one dedicated to a single topic. You should expect this conference to have a wide variety of people and subjects to interest you.

Hawaii International Conference on Education
January 5–8, 2012
Honolulu, Hawaii
Submission Deadline: August 12, 2011

Topic Areas (All Areas of Education Are Invited)

- Academic Advising and Counseling
- Art Education
- Adult Education (Plus 28 other categories)]

Call for Papers, Reports, Abstracts, and Studies:

The Hawaii International Conference on Education encourages the following types of submissions:

- Research Papers
- Abstracts
- Student Papers
- Case Studies
- Work-in-Progress Reports or Proposals for Future Research
- Reports on Issues Related to Teaching

Submitting a Proposal:

1. Create a title page for your submission. The title page should include:
   a. title of the submission
   b. topic area of the submission (choose from the list)
   c. presentation format (choose from the list)
   d. name(s) of the author(s)
   e. department(s) and affiliation(s)
   f. mailing address(es)
   g. e-mail address(es)
   h. phone number(s)
   i. fax number(s)
   j. corresponding author if different from lead author

2. E-mail your abstract and/or paper, along with a title page, to *education@hiceducation.org.*

Plan out the writing and presentation to make sure all important aspects are submitted on time. (iStockphoto.com)

7

The Conference Paper Submittal Timeline

Introduction

The amount of time you will spend between preparing the abstract and presenting your work can be as long as nine months. It can be longer if you start writing your abstract several months before it is due. The timeline can be shorter for many conferences. This chapter guides you through the typical steps, and some optional steps, that some conferences require. Figure 7.1 shows the minimum required phases you must pass through for publishing at a conference.

The following sections discuss the different phases and the approximate time needed for each phase to get your paper published at a conference. An example of a submission process and actual dates are shown in Appendix 7A. Publishing a paper is akin to a journey, and every journey starts with a first step. Generally, the first step is *searching for the right conference.*

Searching for the Right Conference Phase

Time: one week

Finding a conference could take several weeks or months but can be accelerated by the techniques outlined in Chapter 6. You may already know about some conferences from discussions at work, school, your professional society, or from this book. The time to search for a

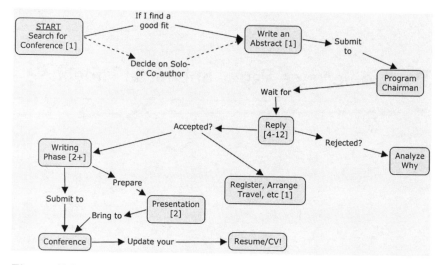

Figure 7.1.
Flowchart of Basic Conference Paper Writing Process (Duration in Weeks)

conference may be zero if you already know your target conference. If not, you might be able to search for and evaluate the conference from the call for papers in one day. The next six days should be spent looking at last year's copy of the conference digest (or other publications from the sponsoring organization) to evaluate if your paper is of the same quality as papers previously published at that conference. This phase could be completed while you are reading your professional society's newsletter or magazine—the call for papers is usually in the last few pages. The right conference could be found quickly, but a key factor is the due date of the abstract. Perhaps you've missed the abstract due date by a month, or this year's conference just finished and the next call for papers will be issued in another six months, but you are ready for next year. Your first conference may require some amount of agonizing, but it gets easier with more experience. See Chapter 6 for the steps required to efficiently evaluate a call for papers.

So, you have found a likely conference, you have thought about it, picked a topic, researched it, and believe that it meets all your requirements—now it's time to start the *abstract phase.*

Abstract Phase

Time: one week

The abstract phase should be short because you probably have the information you need for the abstract. It may be in the summary of a report, in your thesis, in your dissertation, or rattling around in your head. It may not be in the right order to address all the key sections that a scholarly publication requires, and you will have to edit whatever material you have to meet the requirements of the conference (see Chapter 9 for help with writing the abstract). Some abstracts require no more than 150 words, while others (like AERA) require that you submit a 2,000-word summary with very specific requirements addressed in that summary. Write it, read it, rewrite it, have a peer read it, rewrite it, reread it after a few days, and rewrite it again. The abstract is what you are evaluated on—you don't get a second chance!

The abstract phase is complete when you take your abstract and post it to a Web site, or drop it in the mail, *before* the due date. Once you've submitted your abstract, you move on to the *waiting phase.*

Waiting Phase

Time: two weeks to three months (after the abstract deadline)

The waiting time is generally short for simple abstracts (fewer than 500 words). The authors of this book have received acceptances within 24 hours, but that is unusual. Such a quick response usually implies the author's work is well known by the conference committee, and the topic of the abstract meshes well with the theme of the conference. Receiving a notification about four weeks after the *deadline date* is common (not four weeks after you submitted the abstract). Conferences requiring long abstracts or summaries may require more time than usual because the conference peer reviewers will thoroughly review your submission. You should expect to wait as long as three months for a reply.

What if My Abstract Is Accepted?

The waiting phase is finished when the letter or e-mail arrives informing you that your abstract has been accepted or rejected. Key sentences from

SIDEBAR

What if My Abstract Is Rejected?

Don't be discouraged if your abstract was rejected. You have a different set of tasks to accomplish. This is the time to analyze why the abstract was rejected. It could be the abstract did not meet the standards of the conference, the topic did not fit the theme of the conference, it required more editing, or any one of a hundred other possible reasons. The most commonly cited reason is that the conference committee received too many abstracts and had to reject some of the *high-quality submissions*. Acceptance and rejection letters may have phrases like those shown in the Accepted or Rejected? sidebar. Being rejected due to too many abstracts and not enough program slots may actually be the case. However, the reality is that your abstract was rejected, and someone else's abstract was accepted. So, it's time to do some analysis. The analysis phase is very important and may make the difference between being accepted or rejected next time. Strive to understand the rejection of your abstract within one week, but you may have to go to the conference to see your competition and understand why their abstracts were accepted over your abstract. In addition, the rejection letter may have included comments from the reviewers that will help you understand the reasons for rejection.

acceptance and rejection letters to the authors of this book are provided in the sidebar (Accepted or Rejected)—yes, the authors of this book have received several rejection letters! At this point, you have more work to do, but that work certainly differs depending on which letter you receive. If your paper was accepted, go straight to the next section: "Writing Phase." If your paper was rejected, you need to follow the analysis method in the sidebar.

Again, if your abstract was accepted, then it's time to move into the *writing phase*.

SIDEBAR

Accepted or Rejected?

The following phrases were taken from actual acceptance and rejection notices received by the authors. The titles of the papers, the names of the conferences, and other identifying names have been changed to make the sentences generic. These examples will give you an idea of the range of acceptances and one rejection.

1. Your paper titled "TITLE" has been accepted for presentation at the 28th Annual Conference for the CONFNAME at the HOTEL, March 31–April 2, 20xx. Your presentation is scheduled for...

2. Congratulations! The XYZ Conference is pleased to inform you that your submission, "TITLE," will be scheduled for presentation at the fifth annual CONFNAME Conference to be held from May 26 to May 29, 20xx, in CITYNAME. The decision to accept your submission was based on a review process. The exact time and room of your session will be...

3. Thank you for submitting your paper to the CONFNAME Conference. Your paper has been reviewed and accepted, subject to any required technical, format, or language changes noted by the reviewers. We have enclosed all copies of your paper that have reviewers' comments. Please adhere to the Author's Instructions in the...

4. It is with sincere regret that I must inform you that your submission titled "TITLE" was not accepted for presentation at the 20xx CONFNAME Annual Meeting. We typically have an acceptance rate below 50 percent and we again had a large number of exceptionally high-quality submissions this year, competing for fewer program slots than we had last year. We encourage you to seek outlets for the work you submitted and continue to submit to CONFNAME in the future.

Writing Phase

Time: two weeks (maybe more)

The first step in the writing phase is to carefully read the acceptance letter and attachments. This will tell you important things like when you need to finish writing the article and submit it. More importantly, there is occasionally a review of the abstract that recommends you address a specific topic, clarify a point in the abstract, or (rarely) narrow the scope of the paper. It may also recommend you contact another author for input and add him or her as a co-author if an area of your abstract is weak. The authors recommend that you *seriously* consider all the recommendations in the acceptance letter and address the comments explicitly in your final paper.

The writing phase may take longer if you are starting with a blank piece of paper or blank page on a screen, but you shouldn't be starting research for your paper at this time either. You already did a lot of the work before you wrote the abstract, and you probably have done more work and more writing in the weeks before the abstract was accepted. You should not think you are starting with nothing because you are not starting at ground zero—you have a title, the names of the authors, their affiliation, and at least a 150-word abstract that covers the major parts of the paper. A half a page is already done! Co-authors are discussed further in Chapter 8. You may also have a research report from work, a thesis, or a dissertation that you can craft into the paper. Keep the conference-required formatting in mind when you are writing and editing, copying and pasting, and drawing and moving text and artwork. See Chapter 11 for more details on writing the paper.

Don't underestimate the abstract in your paper. It may end up being slightly different than the one you submitted to get accepted to the conference. Writing the abstract is equally as important as writing a legible and accurate paper. The abstract is what will be read by people whenever they look up your paper. With the advent of online searches, people will search for your publications prior to your next job interview. They want to know what is out on the Web about you. Your abstract and paper, and especially your abstract, will say something about you, so you want it to be neat, accurate, and crisp.

SIDEBAR

Wait and Rewriting Phase I (Optional)

Time: four weeks

Some conferences (like most journals) will ask you to rewrite the paper based on editorial and technical content review. This optional phase is quite rare for conferences, but does happen. The revisions are usually minor (add more current references, review and add the impact of a particular significant reference, describe how you reached a particular conclusion, change a table to a figure for clarity, etc.) and require only a few days of work to implement. However, there are times when revisions are extensive and you may want to thoroughly rewrite the paper and submit it to the conference at another time. The rewrite phase I is finished when you submit the final copy of your paper and move into the *rewriting phase 2*.

Some conferences have you submit your paper several months early for a review. This is unusual for a conference, but if it does happen, you want to read the Wait and Rewriting Phase I sidebar on this page.

The writing phase is finished when you submit the final copy of your paper and move to the *preparing for the conference phase.*

Preparing for the Conference Phase

Time: one week

This week is in parallel with the beginning of *preparing the presentation phase* in the next section. This is when you register for the conference, reserve your hotel, and reserve a rental car if needed. This phase finally ends on the day before you leave, when you pack clothes and business cards, locate all your reservation and flight information, and get ready to travel to the conference. This phase may take more time depending on how far in advance the paper is due. In parallel, you should be *preparing the presentation.*

Preparing the Presentation Phase

Time: four weeks

These four weeks are in parallel with the *preparing for the conference* phase above, and this phase is discussed in greater detail in Chapter 12. Don't make the mistake of thinking that your paper is your presentation—they are entirely different beasts. Whether you are experienced at presenting at conferences or it is your first time, many presenters experience feelings of nervousness or self-doubt. Be sure to spend ample time preparing for your presentation, and use the opportunity to experience, learn, and grow. Over time, you will become more and more skilled at presenting. The *preparing the presentation phase* is finished when you get to the conference, pick up your registration package, show up in the right presentation room at the appointed time, and load your presentation on the laptop (and maybe practice). When these two phases are done, you are at the conference and entering the *presentation phase.*

Presentation Phase

Time: (part of) one day

This is what you've been preparing for over the last few months. You've been thinking about this conference, writing an abstract, writing the paper, registering, preparing the presentation, getting a haircut, and traveling to the conference. Now is the time to present your paper—it will be over before you know it. The presentation phase is finished when you sit down after the question-and-answer period and the final round of applause. Take a deep breath and enjoy it! You may still have to pick up extra copies of your handout and check out of the hotel, and get home, but this phase is finished. Congratulations! Once you have mastered the art of presenting at conferences, remember to encourage and support others struggling with presentations.

Many conferences publish the conference digest and have it available at the conference in order to have everyone read/skim the papers the night before or follow along as you are presenting. Having members of the audience either flip through pages of a paper or click though an electronic digest can be distracting to the presenter because the audience is not paying attention

---

SIDEBAR

Rewriting Phase 2

Time: three weeks
There is a trend toward publishing a CD of the papers several months after the conference—allowing authors time to make corrections or adjustments to their papers after receiving feedback from the audience or a discussant. This gives you a second chance to improve your paper or fix that sentence that slipped through without a verb! This rewrite is usually due about three weeks after the conference. Most authors should take advantage of this opportunity to make their paper better. The rewrite phase is finished when you submit the final-final copy of your paper.

---

to the presenter. The audience may be reading ahead, or worse—they are bored and looking at which paper they will attend in the next session.

Some conferences have you submit your paper *after* the conference. This is not unusual for a conference, because it allows you to incorporate comments from the conference. If this is a requirement of the conference, you will want to read the sidebar on this rewriting phase.

Now you are ready to complete the *updating your CV phase.*

Updating Your CV Phase

Time: 10 minutes

If you are like some authors of our acquaintance, you probably updated your CV or résumé as soon as you submitted your abstract and listed the paper as *submitted.* You later changed it to *accepted* when it was accepted. Now you can replace *accepted* with *pages 112–118,* where it is printed in the conference digest. It certainly looks good! An example of a submission process and actual dates are shown in Appendix 7A. Following the conference, you may want to start updating your paper and turn it into a peer-reviewed journal article. Day and Gastel (2011) have written an excellent book on the subject of submitting technical papers to journals.

> Articles can and should emerge from conference papers and often don't. (Bucholtz 2010)

Summary

This chapter walked you through the timeline for submitting a conference paper—from identifying a conference to actual presentation, the entire process could be as short as a few months. It could also be a year if you identify the right conference but are out of sequence. There are very specific steps or phases to be followed for all conference paper submittals:

- Searching for the Right Conference Phase
- Abstract Phase
- Waiting Phase
- Writing Phase
- Prepare the Presentation Phase
- Preparing for the Conference Phase
- Presentation Phase
- Updating Your CV Phase

These simple steps lead you smoothly through the process. They also change your mindset from *I can't possibly write a conference paper* to *This is simple enough—I think I can do this* to the final step where you can say: *I've published and presented my first conference paper and it was great!* Are you ready? Then it's time to step into Section III of this book and determine whether you should have a co-author, what steps to take to get started with your abstract, and learn by example how others have done it.

Bibliography

Bucholtz, Mary. "Tips for Academic Publishing," http://www.linguistics. ucsb.edu/faculty/bucholtz/sociocultural/publishingtips.html (cited August 1, 2010).

Day, Robert, and Barbara Gastel. *How to Write and Publish a Scientific Paper.* Santa Barbara: Greenwood, 2011.

Appendix 7A

TABLE 7.1
Sample Conference Paper Submission Process with Actual Dates

Date	What Did the Authors Do?
July 15, 2005	The authors searched and found the call for papers for the 2006 Hawaii International Conference on Education. It is on education, and the authors have a research study that was conducted at a school. The authors have about a month to get an abstract together. They look at what is needed—500 words.
August 18, 2005	The abstract is due today. The authors finished the abstract in accordance with Chapter 9 and sent it by e-mail to education@hiceducation.org before the end of the day.
August 19, 2005	The authors get an e-mail telling us the abstract was received and settle down to wait.
September 23, 2005	The authors receive an acceptance of the abstract and begin to write the full paper in accordance with Chapter 11.
September 25, 2005	The authors order some business cards for the conference.
October 15, 2005	The authors are happy with the flow, content, and scholarly level of their paper. They e-mail it to education@hiceducation.org and immediately start thinking about the presentation phase.
November 5, 2005	The authors start doing the charts for the presentation phase in accordance with Chapter 12.
November 12, 2005	The authors make hotel and airline reservations and decide to take a shuttle from the airport to the hotel in lieu of a car rental.
December 27, 2005	The authors finish the charts, make a few handout copies of the charts and paper, make transparencies of the charts. They put a soft copy of the presentation on a USB drive and on CD (can't have enough backup systems!). They practice their presentation for timing and flow.
January 3, 2006	The authors pack bags, handouts, business cards, USB drive, and CD.

(Continued)

TABLE 7.1 (*Continued*)
Sample Conference Paper Submission Process with Actual Dates

Date	What Did the Authors Do?
January 4, 2006	The authors go to the airport, fly to Hawaii, shuttle to the hotel, check in, unpack, go to the conference registration desk, pick up registration materials, look up which room they are presenting in, and go to that room to check out both the room and the audiovisual equipment.
January 7, 2006 Early	One of us goes to the room early and loads the presentation onto the conference computer. The authors check to see that the file opens and the projectors work properly, then go to the speaker's breakfast.
January 7, 2006 A few hours later	The authors show up early to the session, meet the session chair and the other presenters. The authors proudly present the paper, gracefully answer all the questions, and humbly accept the applause.
January 11, 2006	The proud new authors check out of the hotel and head home to update their résumés or CVs.

Section III

My First Steps

The chapters in the previous sections took you through the decision process for your journey into the publishing landscape. They identified some of the reasons that you might want to publish at a conference and how to budget the expected costs and time. These three chapters walk you through the next phases of your journey into the publishing landscape.

8. Do I Author the Paper Alone and Who Would Help Me?

9. How Do I Start?

10. Genesis of Some Papers

Chapter 8 addresses the concept of solo authorship versus multiple authorship, how to go about finding co-authors, and includes examples of different types of conference papers that have been presented. Chapter 9 discusses the abstract submission and reminds you that you don't need to write the paper today. You just need to have a catchy title, a list of authors, and the abstract. Examples of published abstracts are given. Chapter 10 gives a few vignettes from the authors' experience in publishing conference papers and how they were conceived. Let's get started by thinking about co-authors.

Collaborating with co-authors is often the most successful option.
(© Dmitriy Shironosov | Dreamstime.com)

8

The Solo-Authoring or Co-Authoring Decision

Take a moment and reflect on who might be of assistance to you during your publishing pursuits.

Introduction

When you publish, you can choose to do it alone or with a co-author. Choosing to solo-author or co-authoring depends on a number of factors. Have you ever published before? Have you published with a reputable journal or conference? Are you working on a project with others who have contributed significantly to the topic of your paper? Do you want to publish alone (solo-authorship) or would you like to co-author a paper with other contributors and share the credit? If you are new to publishing and would rather not go it alone, there are probably several potential co-authors available to you. This chapter will help you decide whether you want to work alone or with co-authors; each has its advantages and disadvantages.

Solo-Authorship or Not?

There are several advantages and disadvantages to publishing a conference paper alone—and vice versa for co-authoring.

Advantages of Solo-Authorship

Working alone on a paper for publishing has several advantages. If your personality leads you to work alone and you do not wish to be bound by others' timelines, solo-authorship is most likely a better choice for you. You can develop your own timeline to meet deadlines, work at your own pace, and be held accountable only to yourself for your success, or lack thereof, in completing your paper for submittal to a conference. Solo-authoring also allows you to make all decisions in terms of style, topic choices, what content to include, and autonomy in choice of references. A solo-authored conference paper acceptance in a top-level conference allows you to take full credit and earns respect from your peers and potential employers. You should solo-author if you have done all the research yourself.

Disadvantages of Solo-Authoring

Working alone on a paper for publishing also has its disadvantages. If you are pressed for time, you may never get your paper finished to meet conference deadlines without the assistance of one or more co-authors. Also, it can be quite helpful to have several writers working on a paper, generating information and ideas, and keeping everyone on track. Co-authors can provide a support network and can create a sense of urgency in one another to drive the paper to successful completion. Several co-authors can bring different strengths to composing a conference paper and presentation. One author might be an excellent writer, another might be an excellent researcher, and another might be an excellent presenter. Together, you learn from one other and create a winning conference paper and presentation. Working alone also forces you to make all decisions in terms of style, topic choices, what content to include, and choice of references. Finally, a poorly prepared solo-authored conference paper or presentation in a top-level conference could be devastating to your career—you alone bear the sole responsibility for mistakes, gaffes, typos,

> When you publish, you can choose to do so alone or with a co-author.

lack of political correctness, and violations of the laws of nature. The authors' opinion about co-authoring is that it is a bit like marriage: it's not 50/50; each half has to give 100 percent. The final disadvantage of solo-authoring is that you fail to build relationships with co-authors that enable you to work on additional projects that could be beneficial to your career in the future.

Case Study. Fran, a second-year doctoral student, decided to take the plunge to rewrite and submit a research paper she had written for her ethics course to a management conference in Las Vegas. Fran checked out the conference Web site, read the requirements, and believed her paper to be a good fit for the conference with a more detailed literature review and some rewriting of several sections. Having never published for a conference, Fran was not sure how to seek help with her first publishing attempt. Initially, Fran decided to scrap the conference. She was taking two courses, had a 10-year-old at home, worked full-time, and thought it just wasn't possible. However, in class, her professor encouraged all students to occasionally publish at least one high quality paper. Fran was smart and approached her professor for some guidance. She submitted her paper, it was accepted, she successfully presented her first paper several months later at the conference, met lots of people in her field, was encouraged to continue her research, and enjoyed a few days in Las Vegas.

Who Could You Get to Help?

Help can come in a variety of forms. It can be guidance, passing advice, a review, or a full co-author. An example of passing advice led to this book. One of the authors was discussing his publishing work and it was casually said, "You ought to write a book." Here are some ideas for people that you know, and some that you might not know (yet), who could help you.

Collaboration of Co-Authors

The collaboration of this book's authors began in classrooms, expanded to conferences and journals, and eventually developed into this book.

Professors

Professors are an excellent and (relatively) easily accessible resource to guide you in publishing a paper. If your professor shares an interest in a topic of your passion, ask the professor if he or she would like to co-author a paper with you. Do not take it personally if a professor turns you down; they are frequently working on research of their own, your topic may not interest them, they may have nothing to contribute, or the timing may not work for them. Professors can also give you hints or suggestions on your topic and may even offer to review your paper prior to submission to the conference. *Hint:* Professors who do not have tenure (those with titles like assistant professor) might be more interested in co-authoring with you.

Classmates

Classmates can be a very easily accessible and eager resource to help you in getting a paper published. If you have a classmate you enjoy working with or who offers a different strength or knowledge base than you have on a similar topic of interest, consider approaching him or her to collaborate on publishing and presenting at a conference. Classmates are often a good resource for connecting you to other sources of information. Frequently, your classmates are willing to review your paper and provide you with comments. They may, in turn, ask you to review their submissions. An excellent example of this is the book that you hold in your hands. The collaboration of this book's two authors began in classrooms, expanded to conferences and journals, and eventually developed into this book.

Business Colleagues

When researching conferences, you may find a conference or topic of interest that relates to your industry or your current employment. If so, you might have some colleagues interested in providing you with information that will further best practices at work or provide alternative solutions for issues facing your organization. A successful paper with real-life benefits for work could lead to a promotion for you. Also, if you and a couple of coworkers finished a research project at work, you may have the basis for a conference paper. Several examples are presented in the next major section (see "Examples of Co-Authored Papers").

Relatives

Another often-overlooked resource is your family. Many people have relatives who are in the teaching profession, may have several publications, and may be able to help you. A popular personality test call the Myers-Briggs Type Indicator (MBTI) was developed by Katharine Cook Briggs and Isabel Briggs Myers, who were mother and daughter respectively. Another well-known team is Frank and Lillian Gilbreth who did motion studies in the 1910s. There are many other instances where relatives, such as a husband and wife, have collaborated on research. There are instances where research collaborators have become husband and wife. However, there may also be examples where collaboration of husband and wife researchers may have led to divorce.

Professional Associations

Co-authors can be found in professional associations and clubs you join. These are the people who have the same interests as you do, and probably go to the same conferences. You may identify another researcher who complements your own research at your next conference.

Conference Contacts

Even if you have never published, you can attend conferences and visit conference Web sites for guidance in submitting your paper. Web sites may also provide past proceedings that allow you to browse, and your reviewing of top-level papers from previous conferences can raise the bar for your paper. If you have already had the opportunity to attend one or two conferences, the authors hope you were able to collect dozens of business cards and make some new acquaintances. These contacts can become co-authors, or they can be a great resource when you have questions, are experiencing writer's block, or just want to talk about your upcoming conference.

During one conference, one of the authors' friends was the third presenter in the session and attentively listened to the two previous papers. She incorporated some of the comments and results that they presented by showing similarities and contrasts in her paper presentation. Afterward, one of the authors of the previously presented papers sought her out and discussed collaborating on a future paper where their results could be merged and expanded upon. This is one example where the co-author finds you. But, as this section described, there are co-authors everywhere around you.

Examples of Co-Authored Papers

Conference papers should provide new and interesting information, but they do not necessarily need to qualify you for a Nobel Prize. Some papers can seem quite ordinary to you, but they must be of some interest to the conference organizers and, eventually, to the participants. This section describes some papers that the authors thought were ordinary but were interesting to others. Collaboration on conference papers often starts at work. In this section, the authors will describe different types of papers that may be interesting to certain conference participants.

The How-We-Did-It Paper

Work on the design of a ground station resulted in the following paper by Mallette and Kelly Knox (two coworkers at the same company and on the same project). This is an example of a *how-we-did-it* paper.

"Power Combining and Signal Routing in the Galaxy TT&C Earth Station." International Telemetering Conference Proceedings, Los Angeles, California, September 1982, 673–680.

The Lessons-Learned Paper

Many papers fall into the *lessons learned* category. Problems and how they were resolved may be of interest to people who have not had the time, experience, or money to investigate an issue. One problem that we wrote an article about was an electronic assembly that had stopped working but fixed itself. The problem is that the electronic assembly is forever tainted—because it might fail again. The following paper, by Mallette and Joel Varney (two coworkers from two different companies but on the same project), was the result of an investigation to identify the root cause of a failure and the steps taken to ensure it would not happen again.

"One Time Transient Failure Investigation." IEEE Aerospace Applications Conference Proceedings, February 1994, 367–371.

The Progress Paper

A popular style for conferences is the *progress paper,* which describes the activities on a project at a point in time. The following paper, by Bhaskar, Hardy, Mallette, and McClelland (coworkers from multiple companies), addressed the status of a project immediately prior to the launch of an electronic assembly into space. As such, there was test data from the ground testing, but no results from the future testing in space.

"Rubidium Atomic Frequency Standards for the MILSTAR Satellite Payload." AIAA Space Programs and Technology Conference Proceedings, San Diego, California, September 1995.

The Final-Results Paper (I)

Many papers are *final results papers* that present the research results at the end of a project, investigation, study, or survey. *Progress papers* such as the one in the previous example may lead to *final results* papers. The following paper, by Bhaskar, Hardy, Mallette, and McClelland (coworkers

---

Content of Conference Papers

Conference papers should provide new and interesting information, but they do not necessarily need to qualify you for a Nobel Prize.

from multiple companies), presented the results of the research once it was complete.

"Rubidium Locked Oscillator Life Testing." IEEE Aerospace Applications Conference Proceedings, February, 1996.

The Final-Results Paper (II)

Another example of a paper from the *final results* category is by Mallette, Tom Folk, and Jim Ulmer (coworkers at the same company), where they presented the results of the research once it was complete.

"Unwanted Microwave Oscillator Frequency Shifts Induced by BJT Die Attach." IEEE Aerospace Applications Conference Proceedings, February 1996.

The Perception Paper

Many papers are *perception papers* that present the research results of a qualitative investigation or survey. They sometimes include excerpts from the participants (flavor bites). The following paper, by Evans, Mallette, and Schmieder-Ramirez (students and professor), presented the results of a survey.

"Perceptions of Doctoral Students Before and After Study in Two Latin American Countries." Hawaii International Conference on Education, Honolulu, Hawaii, January 2005.

The How-To Paper

Many papers are *how-to papers* that are experiential and present a plan or step-by-step instructions. The following paper by Mallette and Michael Moodian (who met at a conference) presented the results of work they had done independently.

"A Neighborhood in the Publishing Landscape: Book Editing." Society of Educators and Scholars Conference, Las Vegas, Nevada, March 2007.

The Review Paper

Some papers are *review papers* that summarize the work of others to date. You would use this format if you published a summary of the literature review from your dissertation. The following paper by Mallette, Pascal Rochat, and Joe White (three experts in their field from different companies, but not coworkers) combined their knowledge and presented a review of the research they and others had done.

> "Historical Review of Atomic Frequency Standards Used in Satellite Based Navigation Systems." Institute of Navigation 2007 Conference, Cambridge, Massachusetts, April 2007.

The Sales Brochure Paper [Example of a BAD Paper]

Some papers are no more than a *sales brochure* or a *press-release paper* summarizing a product or service offered by a company or individual. These are generally not considered a paper for publishing in the conference proceedings and *sales brochure* papers should *never* be submitted as a research-oriented paper at a conference. Sales brochure presentations (the authors are reluctant to call them *papers*) may have a place in certain conferences where there is an exhibits area and each company that is exhibiting is given a very short amount of time (maybe five minutes) to introduce their company and their latest product release. An example of a *press-release* paper (if the authors were so inclined) that would be rejected might be:

> "New Book Released: Writing for Conferences." A Technical Conference, Anytown, Arkansas, December 2011.

Co-Author Labor Split

Instead of the expected 25/25/25/25 percent split, it usually becomes an 80/80/40/20 split.

This section gave examples of different types of papers that you might consider for submission conferences. Whether you choose to author alone or co-author with others, you can always find free resources for assistance.

Other Resources

If you are truly uncomfortable in approaching these individuals or they do not have the time to help you at the moment, you may need to go solo. You can seek help in university libraries, attend writing workshops, surf online Web sites, or purchase books that can provide information to help you complete your paper and presentation.

How Many Co-Authors?

There is a trend away from solo authorship. However, it is best if you don't include everyone who walked past you during your study. There are papers that have been published with 101 co-authors (Seryi et al. 2007). This may be justified, but is extremely unusual. Although many people may have participated in the study, your survey, or a lab experiment, you do not have to include all of them. Include only the ones that have significantly contributed to the research and to producing the conference paper and its presentation. It is common to acknowledge the work of the non–co-authors in the paper—Porco et al. (2005, 167) had three dozen authors and acknowledged an additional seven people in her paper. If your paper is based on work performed by several people, then you should offer each of the report authors an opportunity to contribute in authoring the conference paper.

Professor Ramsey of Tufts University has thought about dissertation student authorship and author order. He published his thoughts online and the authors felt that it was a nice summary. Professor Ramsey has graciously allowed us to reprint his summary in Appendix 8A.

The authors have found that solo-authoring is good, two or three authors can work well together, but having more than three authors can get unwieldy. Instead of the expected 25/25/25/25 percent labor split, the authors have found that it usually becomes an 80/80/40/20 split, or some other inequitable ratio of participation (the effort always adds up to more than 100 percent).

Summary

Are you still wondering if you can find help with publishing your paper? If so, go back and read this chapter again. If you prefer to work with co-authors, there are often resources very close to you (whether it's your professors, classmates, business colleagues, or past conference associates) who would be honored to help you publish. If you find more comfort in publishing on your own, then do so. It is really your own personal preference if you did the all research yourself. The authors have found a variety of sources that could help you, in addition to this book (of course), including:

- Conference Web Sites
- Libraries for Research
- Workshops on Presentation Skills
- Classes on Writing
- Books and Prior Conference Digests

Bibliography

Porco, Carolyn C., et al. "Imaging of Titan from the Cassini Spacecraft." *Nature* 434 (10) (2005): 159–168.

Ramsey, Norman. "Authors," http://www.cs.tufts.edu/~nr/students/guide.pdf (cited October 29, 2009).

Seryi, A., et al. "Design of the Beam Delivery System for the International Linear Collider." Proceedings of 22nd Particle Accelerator Conference, New Mexico, June 25–29, 2007, 1985–1987.

Appendix 8A

Authorship

Used with permission from Professor Norman Ramsey (2009) of Tufts University.

Authorship is the most important form of credit in the academic world. All researchers employed in whatever capacity should be able to expect authorship credit for their contributions. Here, in no particular order, are some thoughts about authorship.

- For a student working on a project under my guidance, the authors expect that the typical case is that the authors write a joint paper with the student as first author. The authors expect such a student to put in substantial work on the manuscript as well as the project. The authors have worked with students who identified and solved problems on their own, with little or no technical support from the research group or the shared infrastructure. When this kind of work is submitted for publication, the student is the sole author—even when the mentors advise the student, it would be inappropriate for them to be a coauthor.

- For a major group project that spans several years, students or others may make significant contributions without taking on major responsibilities for the project. Most often these contributions take the form of implementation work. It is important that these contributions be recognized with authorship credit, but such authors will typically be listed last.

- A student who joins a project already in progress might or might not wind up as a coauthor—it depends on the contribution the student makes.

- When two or more people share major responsibility for a project or a paper, it is usually obvious who should be the "senior" author—that is, the first-named author. If it is not obvious, it falls to the junior or second-named author to make this clear, for example, by saying "I think you should be the lead author on this paper."

- If other things are equal, when a junior person works with senior people, the junior person should be the first author. When faculty work jointly with a student, the student should be first author unless there is a good reason otherwise.

- Don't overlook past contributions of someone who has moved on to another lab by the time a paper is submitted; such people still deserve authorship credit. I have been on both ends of this mistake, and it is one people remember for a long time.

Whether on paper or computer, authors start by writing an abstract. (iStockphoto.com)

9

Starting the Writing: The Abstract

You start by writing an abstract.

Introduction

You have identified a conference, and your topic fits perfectly. This is your opportunity to start writing your first paper. *So what's holding you back?*

Are you worried it won't get accepted? So what? You'll be one of many who won't get accepted. Nobody cares. Swallow your pride, learn from it, and you'll do better next time.

Are you worried it *will* get accepted?

(Oh no! That means you'll have to write a conference paper in addition to that analysis that is due for statistics, and you're planning a weekend getaway with your family, and your job is really busy, and you have to mow the lawn, and groceries are getting low, and you might have to wash the car, and you've been meaning to balance your checkbook, and you want to paint the spare bedroom before your in-laws arrive next summer, and...) *Stop.*

Yes, *stop*. Life is full of stuff, and you need to make the decision that you're going to do the work if your paper gets accepted. It may not hurt to start thinking about the paper before you get that acceptance letter and possibly do some writing.

Many people start with an outline of what they want to talk about. Most outlines have the following framework:

- Title block
- Abstract
- Introduction
- Body of paper: topics one to three (or more)
- Conclusions
- References

Chapter 11 will discuss the last four of these sections of the conference paper, but the title block and abstract are submitted first. So, let's review them.

The Title Block and Abstract

The abstract as submitted for consideration by the conference program committee should be a microcosm of the paper, giving an introduction, discussing the contents, and summarizing the key results.

Paper Is not Necessary at This Time

Remember, most conferences want a short abstract. They usually require 150 to 300 words. Some conferences request additional material that could include a 2,000-word summary, but these are rare. You don't need to write the paper today. You just need to have a catchy title, a list of authors, and the abstract. The title block includes the actual title of the paper and the author information.

Catchy Title. The word *catchy* is not meant to imply bizarre, tabloid-esque, eye-catching headlines. But it is more appealing to the reader if the

> Abstract. You don't need to write the paper today.
> You just need to have a catchy title, a list of authors, and the abstract.
> Put your name below the title in the way you want it to be seen forever.

TABLE 9.1
Examples of Poor and Better Titles for Articles

Poor Titles	Better Titles
Habits of Sphenisciformes	Management Techniques of the King Penguin
Alternate Switching Behavior in the 422 Relay	Sneak Circuit Paths That Can Bite You
How Mice Learn Management Behavior	Who Moved My Cheese?
A qualitative review of the investigation of the individuals in 1960 to 1969 to whom (blah, blah, blah)	Promiscuity During the Beatles Decade
An Interdisciplinary Analysis Methodology Using the Social, Political, Environmental, Legal, Intercultural, and Technological Environments	The SPELIT Power Matrix

title draws in the reader emotionally. Examples of poor and better titles are presented in Table 9.1.

List of Authors. Immediately below the title will be the list of authors. If you are solo-authoring, then this is a simple list. Put your name below the title in the way you want it to be seen forever. This may require more thought than you might initially think. This is the name that search engines will save (forever), and future searchers will only find you by that name. Do you want to use your full first name, an abbreviated first name, an initial, or a nickname? The first author of this book could use Leo or L. or Lee (he has never used Lee, but it's a possibility). You may want to ask yourself if you want to use your middle initial or full middle name. If you have a very common name, then adding the middle letter or middle name makes it more distinguishable (and searchable). On the other hand, do you want the world to know your middle name is Aloysius or Hortense? Remember that when people do a search for you in the future, they will find you and your middle name. If you use this name, you should use the same name for *all* future publications—this may be for the next 50 years! When people are searching for this book's primary author's papers, they have to search for any of the following: Leo Mallette, Leo A. Mallette,

L. Mallette, or L. A. Mallette. It would be nice if one search would find all of his publications.

Author Order Protocol. One closely related issue to ethics is the author-order protocol. The first named author of a multiple-author article is often referred to as the lead or senior author and the other(s) as the junior author(s). This discussion was started in Appendix 8A and is continued here. The lead author is usually the one who presents the paper.

The authors can be listed by quantity of contribution, alphabetically, or some other formula. For example, the author with the greatest name recognition is sometimes listed last. "Among [Nobel] laureates, first authorship is taken on only 26 percent of collaborative papers" (Bayer and Smart 1991, 616) in an attempt to offset the *Matthew Effect,* which is the phenomena (named after a verse in the biblical Gospel according to Matthew, 25:29–30) where a well-known, famous, or senior author will get more credit than a lesser-known author (Merton 1968, 56), regardless of position in the list of authors. This is often a personal preference of the authors or can be dictated by the department within the university.

Non-Contributors. In no cases should authors be added if they did not contribute to the research or writing. Examples of people who might want to be included, but shouldn't be included if they didn't contribute, are the lab manager who provided lab space, your advisor if he did not contribute to the paper, the sponsor of your research (providing funds is not the same as performing research), or the department chairman (because he wants to go visit his grandkids in the city where the conference is being held). The authors of this book recommend listing authors either alphabetically or by percent of contribution to the research and writing; with the presenting author listed first.

Address. Conferences usually require affiliation and contact information. The title block is good place to put that information if there are no specific directions otherwise. Use your work address and e-mail address. Yes, your work address may change, but your home address may change too. This is a professional paper, and you want to show your professional affiliation and address. Your university or business (especially if they pay for some of the costs) want you to acknowledge your affiliation with them. Author Mallette has used home, school, and business addresses and home

---

SIDEBAR

Thought Experiment

Consider the research you are doing at this time. First read aloud the following sentence beginnings, completing them appropriately for your research.

1. I have done research on _____ .

2. Other researchers have found _____ .

3. The problem is _____ .

4. The question I am trying to answer is _____ .

5. This is important because _____ .

6. The research method I used was _____ .

7. I found _____ and _____ .

8. I also found _____ .

9. This implies _____ .

   You've just mumbled about 200 words. Now write those words down, include the numbers for the results, eliminate the passive tense, eliminate the personal pronouns, and you have got a rough abstract.

---

and work e-mail addresses at one time or another—he gets e-mail at several addresses, and it is sometimes confusing.

The title block was easy (the catchy title, the list of authors, affiliation, and the address). Now it's time to start on the abstract.

Abstract

Outline. Type the word *Abstract* below the title block and center it. Many people start writing an abstract by following the outline of what they want to discuss in the paper. The abstract should be a microcosm of the paper, giving an introduction, discussing the contents, and summarizing the key results (or hinting at what the key results will be).

One of the scholarly methods for writing papers is to follow the format for a social sciences dissertation. The first chapter in most dissertations is the introduction. The second dissertation chapter is the review of the literature. The first two chapters are almost always combined into an introductory section in conference and journal articles. The third dissertation chapter is a description of the research methods used and why these are valid. The fourth dissertation chapter is a statement of the results of your research. This is where the statistics are presented. The fifth dissertation chapter is a discussion of the results and tying the results back to the literature.

This is also an effective approach for an abstract. You could write two sentences each on the introduction, background, and methods, and three or four sentences on the result. You will find that this approach will easily yield 125 words, and you may find yourself having trouble keeping within the conference's word limit for the abstract. This would be a good time to try the experiment in the Thought Experiment sidebar. Following are some examples of abstracts from published papers by the authors and discussions of those abstracts.

Example of an Abstract for a Consultation Results Paper

Organizational Analysis Tools to Identify Possible Cause and Corrective Action for Lack of Collaboration between Principals in a Private School

This paper describes an investigative process used to help identify the possible cause of a problem and develop recommendations based on findings, ultimately improving the quality of education for students and educators. The executive director of a private K-8 school identified a need to increase administrative staff in year 2000. Due to an increase in enrollment and added faculty, an additional principal was hired, and a reorganization of duties occurred resulting in one elementary principal and one junior high principal overseeing the education program. The principals had different leadership styles and were unwilling to work collaboratively with each other. As a result, teacher morale and retention were negatively impacted, and parents noted a problem in students transitioning from elementary school to junior high school. A pro bono consulting team from Pepperdine University consisting of four doctoral students studying education and organizational leadership was asked to evaluate the situation, identify the problem, and provide recommendations to improve or resolve the situation. The consultants used several investigative and planning tools to identify the root cause of the problem and provide proper corrective action for the situation. These tools included team brainstorming, Mager and Pipe Performance Analysis Flowchart and Worksheet (Mager and Pipe 1997), a survey, histogram, fishbone analysis, Pareto chart, radar chart, interrelationship digraph, and prioritization. A logical investigation process found the main issue to be a lack of collaboration between principals. Final recommendations provided by the consulting team included contracting with an outside facilitator to improve communications between the principals, requiring faculty members to take a larger role (ownership) to determine what is required for retention purposes, and creating a transition plan for students. (Berger, Evans, Mallette, and Suwandee 2005, 1357)

The preceding 273-word abstract immediately describes the type of investigation this paper discusses. The reader will either be interested and read on or move to another abstract. The problem is stated, the investigation methodology and tools used are described, and the brief results are presented. The abstract was accepted and the paper associated with this abstract was presented at a conference in Hawaii in 2005.

Example of an Abstract for a Review Paper

Atomic and Quartz Clock Hardware for Space Applications

Accurate and stable frequency reference sources are critical for commercial, navigation, military, and scientific space applications. For any piece of flight hardware, there are many requirement-types that are generic (weight, power, size, reliability, etc), and unique (output power, noise figure, axial ratio, gain, throughput, capacity, group delay, etc.), but the key requirements for reference sources are phase noise and stability. There are several levels of frequency references suitable for space applications. This paper will discuss similarities and differences of single distributed oscillators as used in many communications satellites, master oscillators used in military systems, and atomic clocks for military and navigation systems. The future of space clocks are briefly discussed, including the chip-scale atomic clock progress. (Mallette 2007, 57)

The preceding 116-word abstract immediately states the importance of the review paper and then mentions what other researchers consider important. It closes with the methods that will be used to present the findings of this review paper. The paper associated with this abstract was presented at a conference in California in 2007.

Example of an Abstract for an Investigation Results Paper

Correlation of Frequency Hopped VCO Phase Settling to Varactor Transient Capacitance

Microwave VCO and system designers should be aware that attoFarad level changes in the dynamic performance of a varactor can correlate to changes in system settling response of fast hopping frequency synthesizers. It is theorized that a moisture/silicon interaction occurred within a packaged varactor diode due to imperfect wafer processing of the die and a flawed ceramic enclosure. The flawed ceramic allowed ambient moisture to penetrate and come in contact with exposed silicon at the surface of the die junction, causing an increase in interface (or surface) states which in turn increased the settling time constant of diode capacitance on the order of fifty microseconds. The increased time constant was correlated to an observed degradation in VCO phase settling. (Mallette, Delaney, Killman, Folk, and Wong 1999, 1133)

The preceding 119-word abstract immediately states the results of the investigation and entices the technical reader with the rarely seen term *attoFarad*. The theory and methodology of the investigation are stated, and the results of the testing are very specifically and quantitatively expressed. The paper associated with this abstract was presented at a conference in France in 1999.

Next Steps

The next steps are to proofread your abstract, submit it to the conference, confirm it was received, sit back, and either wait or start working on the paper. It's hard to keep from thinking about how you will write the paper. Little snippets of perfect wording will appear in your head and demand to be written down. You will find ways to improve your abstract, and before you know it, a letter or an e-mail will arrive, communicating either acceptance or rejection of your submitted abstract. There are two paths to follow once you receive the notification.

When Accepted

This is when you will be required to devote time and money to your effort. Until now, it took some time to prepare the abstract, but your time commitment and costs were probably minimal.

Time. Now you will have to perform the research (if it is not done), write the paper, make travel and hotel reservations, prepare slides for the presentation, travel to the conference, and present the paper. All of this will take time. The amount of time required is discussed in more detail in Chapter 7.

Money. This is the time when you will be using your (or the company's) credit card to make travel arrangements and hotel reservations and to register for the conference. All of these will cost money and generally need to be done ahead of time. You definitely don't want to show up to an out-of-town conference and not have a hotel room waiting for you. The estimated amount of money required was discussed in detail in Chapter 3.

If Rejected

You will get some rejections. Although you may be tempted to use the popular technique of Figure 9.1, the authors caution you to resist. You

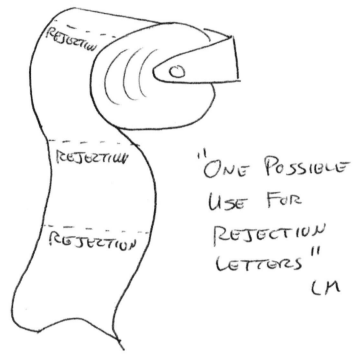

Figure 9.1.
Your Possible Initial Reaction to the Receipt of a Rejection Letter

must take the rejection letter and learn from it, fix your submission, and resubmit it to another conference.

Status Tracking Tool

A list is an important reference tool to keep track of your paper. The template in Figure 9.2 is used by the authors to keep track of their paper submission(s). The descriptions of individual lines are explained in Appendix 9A and two samples of completed forms are shown in Appendices 9B and 9C. This template provides one easy-to-access file that has relevant information in one place. It is better than searching for multiple paper or electronic files or Web sites every time you have a question about an important date. This type of tool is especially important when there is significant

Short Title: *Paper Name*
Conference: *Name*
Date: *Date(s)*
Location: *Hotel or Convention Center, City, Country*

Task	Due Date	Comment
Abstract		
Acceptance		
Paper Clearance		
Paper		
Copyright Release Form		
Presentation		
Registration		
Hotel		
Air Travel		
Notes		

Figure 9.2.
Summary Table Template for Tracking Progress, Examples in Appendices 9B and 9C

time between submissions of abstracts and acceptances of papers. You can staple this form to the inside of your paper file folder where you keep your work in progress or place it in the electronic file folder on your laptop. Remember that there is nothing magic about this form. You can adapt it any way you want, as long as you don't miss a submission deadline!

This section and the accompanying appendices discussed the need for tracking your progress and provided a reference template that could be used as a checklist with specific due dates; providing one easy-to-access file that has relevant conference information in one place.

Ethical Responsibilities
An entire chapter could be devoted to this subject, but the authors have sprinkled ethical ideas throughout this book. We discussed ethical responsibilities of the author(s); specifically in Chapter 4 (responsibility to

register and present the paper if it is accepted). Plagiarism should always be avoided (give proper credit to authors who you used) and self plagiarizing is discussed in Chapter 4 and this chapter (the 50 Percent Rule). Do not submit the same abstract to multiple conferences and then down-select the one you like best. Author contribution, order, and protocol was discussed previously in this chapter. Some of these ethical ideas are fleshed out in more detail in the next paragraphs.

Write, Register, and Present

There are a few rules to remember about writing for conferences:

1. Write the paper if you get accepted.

2. At least one author should register for the conference.

3. Attend the conference on the day of your presentation.

4. Present a paper that is not a rehash of a paper from another conference.

Write the paper if you get accepted. If your abstract is accepted, commit to writing the paper and submit it on time.

At least one author should register for the conference. Conferences do not magically happen—the rooms, projectors, and meals are paid for by your registration fees. One of the authors should pay the registration fee and attend.

Attend the conference on the day of your presentation. People are interested in your topic and will show up to hear you speak. This may be your first step in the job interview process.

Present a paper that is not a rehash of a paper from another conference. Obviously, if you are an expert in a field and you write several papers, you will be writing about the same subject. It is hard to not use a few sentences from a previous paper, especially the review of the literature, which doesn't change much. A personal rule the authors try to use to meet

---

Offer an abstract in haste, repent in leisure. (Neal Brune, personal communication, 2007)

the requirements of Rule 4 is the 50 Percent Rule: Ethically, the paper must be new. To this end, the authors recommend that the text, content, and artwork must change at least 50 percent in order to qualify as a new paper. This was discussed in more detail in Chapter 4.

Another rule that usually shouldn't need to be mentioned is about plagiarism. If you use someone else's words, you must give them credit. That's what you would expect them to do with your words. Right?

Summary

This chapter asked, "What's holding you back from writing your abstract?" It discussed the fear of rejection and the fear of acceptance and pointed out that a catchy title and an abstract are all that is needed. Writing an abstract or an outline to create an abstract were discussed, selecting a co-author if desired, and the steps required after your paper is accepted or rejected were reviewed. Several ethical considerations associated with publishing were mentioned.

Bibliography

Bayer, Alan, and John Smart. "Career Publication Patterns and Collaborative 'Styles' in American Academic Science. *Journal of Higher Education* 62 (6) (1991): 613–636.

Berger, Clare, Leslie Evans, Leo Mallette, and Atit Suwandee. "Organizational Analysis Tools to Identify Cause and Corrective Action for Lack of Collaboration between Principals in a Private School." Hawaii International Conference on Education, January 2005.

Merton, Robert K. "The Matthew Effect in Science." *Science* 159 (3810) (1968): 56–63.

Mager, Robert, and Peter Pipe. "Analyzing Performance Problems." Center for Effective Performance, Atlanta, 1997.

Mallette, Leo. "Atomic and Quartz Clock Hardware for Space Applications." 39th IEEE Precise Time and Time Interval Applications Proceedings, November 2007.

Mallette, Leo, Michael Delaney, Steven Killman, Thomas Folk, and Boon Wong. "Correlation of Frequency Hopped VCO Phase Settling to Varactor Transient Capacitance." IEEE Frequency Control Symposium Proceedings, Besancon, France, April 1999, 1133–1137.

Appendix 9A

Summary Table Template for Tracking Progress

Short Title: *Paper Name*

Conference: *Name*

Date: *Date(s)*

Location: *Hotel or convention center, city, country*

Task	Due	Comment
Abstract		
Acceptance		
Paper Clearance		
Paper		
© Release Form		
Presentation		
Registration		
Hotel		
Air/Travel		

Notes:

The first line (*Title or Short Title*) in the top block can contain the full title or a short title to remind you of the topic of this paper or to differentiate it from other papers you may be preparing. Add the full conference name, the dates of the conference, and the location (including the conference venue). All of these are important in your planning for writing and attending the conference. Your matrix may have more (or fewer) rows than shown, depending on the conference requirements. The tasks within the matrix (table) will be updated as you accomplish tasks. The individual lines are described in the next paragraphs.

Abstract. List the date that the abstract is due. You may want to make a note if there are some unusual requirements. Some conferences require a longer summary submitted at the same time as the abstract. Once you've submitted the abstract, make a note of the submittal date and method (mail, e-mail, or hand delivered). If you submitted your paper late, you should have done so with permission of the program chairman—make a note of having talked to her.

Acceptance. List the date that was indicated in the call for papers. If there was no date for acceptance/rejection letters, then ask for an estimated date. Contact the program chairman for status on your submittal if it is two weeks after the promised date and you have not received notification. List the date you received the letter once you receive confirmation that your abstract was accepted. Make a note to yourself if there were any stipulations. For example, your abstract may have been accepted subject to making modifications per a reviewer's comments.

Paper Clearance. Pick a date about a month before the paper is due. If your company doesn't have a requirement to clear the paper before it is published (or your university doesn't have an institutional review board (IRB) publishing requirement), you may want to delete this line. You will need to give your company adequate time to perform this review, and the bigger companies may take several weeks to perform this task. If your paper is cleared by your company, indicate the date it was cleared and how to locate any documentation to prove it (tracking number or e-mail date).

Paper. Indicate when the paper is due. You may not know this until the abstract has been accepted. Once you've submitted the paper, make a note of the submittal date and method (mail, e-mail, or hand delivered). If you submitted late, you should have done so with permission of the program chairman—make a note of having talked to her.

Copyright Release Form. If required, this is due when the paper is due. This is usually important enough to keep as a separate line for this item. Your paper won't get published if you fail to complete this step on time.

Presentation. This should be finished at least a week before you travel to the conference. You don't want to be looking for data or a figure when you're packing and leaving for the airport. Yes, you can fiddle with the words up until the last minute, but the package should be presentable by a week ahead of time. You may want to list if there are special presentation requirements—who knows, maybe the conference won't have laptops with projectors because they can only afford to rent overhead projectors. You could indicate the date, time, and room of your presentation when you get the advanced program.

Registration. List the date where early registration ends. You want to be especially careful with registration since there is often a late registration date when the costs increase. In the comments section, indicate the date you registered, your confirmation number (if any), the cost, your check number, and any other information that would be useful. For example, if you registered for only one day, make a note of the day—you certainly don't want to show up on Thursday with a Tuesday registration.

Hotel. Check the call for papers to find the guarantee date for conference rates. The prices will go up after this date. In the comments section, record the name of the hotel, your confirmation number, the quoted price, how you paid for it, and any other information that would be useful. You may want to list who you talked to when you made the reservation, and if you were told you were getting a nonsmoking room with a king-size bed and a view of the ocean.

Air/Travel. There is not usually a specific deadline for making airline reservations, but you might want to subtract 21 days from your first travel date to get lower airfares (possibly). There may be other travel possibilities, such as driving or taking the train. The authors have found that it is more convenient to drive to most conferences that are within about 200 miles. Sometimes you can plan a weekend vacation before or after the conference, and it's usually nice to have a car. There are an increased number of online conferences, but that defeats (or severely limits) the ability to network with people and touch the products in the exhibit area.

Other. There may be other issues that you want to add at the end. One of them is to verify after the conference that your paper actually did get published in the conference proceedings. This is especially important when the digest is not distributed at the conference, but afterward, in order for authors to incorporate the comments received during the conference. It may take six months after the conference before the digest is distributed.

Notes. This is a good place to list miscellaneous items or those that are too long to put in the table. You might note the Web site for the conference; paste in your airline itinerary; and indicate if you need to bring a raincoat, formal wear, or Hawaiian wear. You may want to look up a relative or an old classmate; this is a good place to put his or her name and contact information.

Appendices 9B and 9C show two examples of this format in use.

Appendix 9B

Example of Completed Summary Table for Tracking Progress of a Paper

Short Title: Publishing rates

Conference: Position location and navigation symposium

Date: April 25–27, 2006

Location: Loews Coronado Bay Resort, San Diego

Task	Due	Comment
Abstract	November 15	Submitted October 15
Acceptance	December	Accepted January 13
Paper	April 3	2 copies and 1 electronic, copyright release
Presentation	April 23	Session D6, April 27, 1 p.m.
Registration	March 20	E-mail receipt 3-13, $425 student rate
Hotel	March 23	3-10, Marlena, $195/night, #3594752
Air/Travel	N/A	N/A
Resubmit	May 5	4-31

Notes:

• http://www.plans2006.org/

The example in this appendix describes a conference about 150 miles away where a hotel was needed, but airfare was listed as *not applicable* because the authors drove to the conference. This example also shows an added line at the end where there was an opportunity to make corrections and resubmit the paper after the conference for the proceedings.

Appendix 9C

Example of Summary Table for Tracking Progress, Showing Two Papers

Short Title: 1000/Landscape

Conference: SES 2007

Date: March 22–24

Location: Las Vegas at UNLV

Task	Due	1,000 Days Paper	Landscape Paper
Abstract	Nov 10	Submitted 9-19	Submitted 9-19
Acceptance	February	Yes	Yes
Paper	Mar 22	March 15	Feb 25
Presentation	Mar 15	Done	Done
Registration	Mar 22	$400, #6131, on Feb 16	Same
Hotel	January	Tahiti Village	Same
Air/Travel	N/A	Drive	Same

Notes:

- March 22 (Thursday) to March 24 (Saturday), 2007, at the Student Union, UNLV Campus, Las Vegas, Nevada
- http://www.ses-online.org

The example in this appendix shows the matrix with an added column being used to track two papers submitted to the same conference. This could have been done with two tables with the second table not needing the *registration, hotel,* and *air/travel* lines. You can see that both abstracts were submitted on the same date, but the two papers were finished on different dates. In this case, the presentations were completed, but the completion dates were not indicated. Similar to the example in Appendix 9B, the authors drove to the conference and did not need air transportation. The venue for the conference was not a hotel, and the conference location was indicated in the *notes* section.

Sometimes ideas for papers practically materialize from your computer.
(iStockphoto.com)

10

Genesis of Some Papers

Nothing does more to further your career than publication. (Clapham 2005, 391)

Introduction
Question: Where do ideas for conference papers come from?
Answer: They come from you.

They are inside you right now. Sometimes these ideas are deeply buried, and sometimes they are on the surface and screaming to get out. Often, they are already out and part of something you have already written. You already have some of the thoughts developed and many of them may be written down in a report for work, an analysis you performed, a survey you did, or a novel approach you thought about and started to record in your planner, PDA, or on your computer. Or the seed of a conference paper may be in your master's thesis or doctoral dissertation. This chapter takes you through some examples of developing a conference article and a few *first article* vignettes from other people.

Publish or Perish
Phil Clapham provides some advice for the newcomer to publishing. Although his advice is for a peer-reviewed journal, the same thoughts apply to conference papers.

Not that the writing of a scientific paper is an easy task for the novice. The late Bill Watkins—legendary for both his science and his red pen—informally reviewed my own first effort, and when the manuscript was returned to me, I thought he had ritually sacrificed some small animal over it. I don't know how many publications went by before the writing of a scientific paper became routine for me, but one day I suddenly realized I was no longer agonizing over structure and content. So take heart: it gets easier with each paper you take on.... Finally, all of you students who are contemplating your future in an uncertain and competitive job market, know this: nothing does more to further your career than publication. Publications say that you are serious about research and can take the scientific process all the way through to completion. I have a rule that I've applied ever since my first publication: always have at least one paper in review at any given time. Keep to that and, in a few years, you will find your curriculum vitae expanding to a surprising extent and with it, your career opportunities. (Clapham 2005, 391)

The authors agree with Clapham's suggestion of one paper in review at any given time, but they have also experienced publishing cycles where writers have peaks and valleys in their writing output (more in Chapter 4). You may not always have a paper in work. Having a paper in the review cycle is good advice, so let's look at a few examples at how others have gotten started on some papers.

Theory Pi

A publishing idea occurred to one of the authors during a class on leadership theory, although the concept had been fermenting in his brain for a long time. He had worked as an aerospace engineer for 30 years and noticed they were often highly motivated but often introverted people. Most leadership theories in the books did not adequately describe his observations. So he developed a theory that attempted to describe this group of people, their behavior at work, and a possible leadership method that could be used to properly lead them. Theory Pi people included highly motivated but introverted people: possibly including some doctoral candidates; scientists in general; and, for the purposes of this conference paper, engineers specifically. It was based primarily on the author's 30 years of being an aerospace engineer and observing aerospace engineers. The paper reviewed the many leadership theories and expanded upon the earlier theories by describing competent but introverted groups such as (some) engineers who are described as an INTJ personality type by the Myers-Briggs Type Indicator (MBTI). These engineers tend to be fiercely self-motivated by their task or project. They tend to be loyal to their field of interest and may only be loosely related to their project's goals. This was not an easy paper to research and write, and he had more questions after he wrote it than when he began. This could lead to more literature search, research, surveys, interviews, and refinement of the theory. The abstract reads as follows:

This paper defines Theory Pi—an attempt to describe a group of people, their behavior at work, and a possible leadership method that can be used to properly lead them. Theory Pi people include highly motivated but introverted people such as doctoral candidates, scientists in general and engineers specifically. It is based on a literature search and 30 years of observing aerospace engineers. This paper reviews the theories of leadership and describes how Theory Pi advances the literature. Theory Pi expands upon the earlier fundamental Theories X and Y by Douglas McGregor and Theory Z by William Ouchi. This is done by describing a theory that provides a clear understanding of the human nature associated with extremely competent but introverted groups such as (some) engineers. These engineers tend to be fiercely self-motivated by their task or project. They tend to be loyal to their field of interest and may only be loosely related to their project's goals. Examples from the literature, and a story from engineer lore, are presented to confirm or disconfirm the author's hypothesis that engineers are different and need to be lead differently. A table juxtaposes Theory Pi with Theories X, Y, and Z. Further research is recommended to provide evidence for the hypothesis. (Mallette 2005, 684)

The authors have found you can get into a rash of publishing, and this sometimes is followed by a slump. While this Theory Pi paper may not have been the author's first conference publication, he had been in a

> Sometimes you get into a rash of publishing, and sometimes you get into a slump.

publishing slump. This was one of his first conference papers in five years, and it got him out of his slump.

Consulting Case Study

A conference paper was conceived when the authors were asked to consult on a study to identify possible causes related to two assistant principals refusing to work collaboratively in a private school. One assistant principal managed the elementary grades and the other managed the middle school. Due to the lack of collaboration, teacher morale and retention were low, and parents complained that students were experiencing difficulty in transitioning from elementary school to junior high. The authors used several investigative tools to identify causes of the problem, including a survey, histogram, fishbone analysis, Pareto chart, radar chart, and interrelationship digraph, among others. The team was prevented from contacting the assistant principals directly, but the faculty were contacted via survey. The main cause appeared to be significantly different leadership styles between the assistant principals. Final recommendations included contracting with an outside facilitator to improve communications between the assistant principals, requiring faculty members to take an ownership role in determining retention requirements, and creating a transition plan for students.

Following the completion of the case study, the authors developed and submitted the abstract of the case-study paper to an educational conference, and it was subsequently accepted (Berger et al. 2005). The conference happened to be the first conference for one of the presenting authors. Upon arriving at the conference, she had the opportunity to attend at least a dozen other conference sessions prior to presenting this paper. By then, the author had been exposed to many different types and styles of presentations and felt much more comfortable and confident about presenting in a session in front of an audience. The conference turned out to be a positive learning experience, and the author moved on to publishing at other conferences. The abstract read as follows:

This paper describes an investigative process used to help identify the possible cause of a problem and develop recommendations based on findings, ultimately improving the quality of education for students and educators. The executive director of a private K-8 school identified a need to increase administrative staff in year 2000. Due to an increase in enrollment and added faculty, an additional principal was hired, and a reorganization of duties occurred resulting in one elementary principal and one junior high principal overseeing the education program. The principals had different leadership styles and were unwilling to work collaboratively with each other. As a result, teacher morale and retention were negatively impacted, and parents noted a problem in students transitioning from elementary school to junior high school. A pro bono consulting team from Pepperdine University consisting of four doctoral students studying education and organizational leadership was asked to evaluate the situation, identify the problem, and provide recommendations to improve or resolve the situation. The consultants used several investigative and planning tools to identify the root cause of the problem and provide proper corrective action for the situation. These tools included team brainstorming, Mager and Pipe Performance Analysis Flowchart & Worksheet (Mager and Pipe 1997), a survey, histogram, fishbone analysis, Pareto chart, radar chart, interrelationship digraph, and prioritization. A logical investigation process found the main issue to be a lack of collaboration between principals. Final recommendations provided by the consulting team included contracting with an outside facilitator to improve communications between the principals, requiring faculty members to take a larger role (ownership) to determine what is required for retention purposes, and creating a transition plan for students. (Berger et al. 2005, 1375)

Using What You Have

It was mentioned to a student friend that a conference was coming up and that she should try to submit an abstract, but the submission deadline was fast approaching. The student said she was too busy to create a new research paper and the professor said, "Why don't you use a research paper you have written for one of your doctoral classes?" He explained that if she did a little enhancement and modification, she could get it to fit into the conference theme. He was right. With very little additional text, the abstract (below), originally focused on recent changes in information and communication technologies, was re-created to reflect the recent changes in connecting the global community with communication technologies. Simple changes, but they resulted in getting accepted by the conference and an opportunity to be published and to share her research with the conference attendees. The abstract read as follows:

> The power of communication technologies to reduce the effects of geographical distance and to contribute to the feeling of being one global village has dramatically increased in the past decade. Advances in satellite communications and the dramatic growth in the availability and capability of information and communication technologies (ICTs) have revolutionized both the speed and nature of global communications (Kirkwood 2001). Global communication involves many new technologies. The most important technology affecting our lives today is the Internet. This technology has brought the benefits of communicating globally within the reach of millions, yet there are still greater numbers for whom this technology is not available. As the United Nations found, "The collapse of space, time, and borders may be creating a global village, but not everyone can be a citizen" (United Nations Development Programme 1999). The purpose of this paper is to explore this digital divide and to recommend an appropriate direction for the future of global communication technology. First, important statistics paint a picture of the scope of the situation. Then examples of programs that try to integrate the many factors involved in advancing global communication are given. Lastly, an overview leaves the reader with a sense of the future direction of the industry. (Evans 2004, 162)

Collaborating with Professionals

An opportunity to collaborate with other authors can arise from your presentation. One of the authors of this book and a friend presented at a management conference and found synergy with an author who presented in the same session. The topics were uniquely connected, the first author talking about monitoring consumers shopping patterns and the second set of authors talking about employers monitoring employees' e-mail in the workplace. The second presentation augmented and reinforced the points that the first author was making. After the session was complete, the author of the first paper asked us if we would be interested in collaborating on an extension of their research, working under the new grant he had received from his university in Australia. This represented a unique opportunity to collaborate on a global scale.

Cows and Salami Slicing

Have you ever thought of a concept, had an outpouring of great ideas, and experienced flashes of insight about how they could be used in many ways or by many groups? There are similar scenarios where you have finished some far-reaching research or have finished a work project that has broad implications. This is the time where your idea, research, project, analysis, thesis, or dissertation can be turned into a conference paper for different types of conferences. This phenomenon, where different aspects of your work can be presented at several different and diverse conferences is called a *cow*. It is referred to as a *cow* because you are taking an idea and *milking* it for every possible idea that can be presented at various conferences. Another term is *salami slicing,* where a research report or dissertation may have many parts to it and could be sliced into several papers.

The authors are not saying that you present the same paper at different conferences: Absolutely not. Instead, different aspects of your work could be presented at various conferences while supporting the same basic premise. Your study on the leadership traits of female penguins could be presented at many conferences. You could discuss the leader-follower patterns at a bird conference, then contrast it with family-owned businesses at a small business conference, and then present a paper on penguin leadership training at an adult learning conference.

The penguin example may be a bit flighty, but consider what you are doing in your work or studies. There could be a financial side to your project at work; a leadership or management theory that you used; a technology that you are creating, adapting, or using for your studies; a human relations or ethical dilemma that you resolved; or a communications problem that you identified and solved. These various, but distinct, topics could be presented at several different specialty and regional conferences.

Vignettes

In order to offer one of the more interesting sections of this book, the authors asked several conference authors to write an interesting and factual story of their first conference publishing experience. The authors value the experience of others and wanted to include their stories in this book.

VIGNETTE

Multiple Papers from a Master's Thesis

Leo Mallette, Author

A friend stated that I *milked* my master's thesis. I worked on the project and the thesis writing for many months and was convinced by my advisor that publishing this work would be worthwhile. So, I presented the basic idea and the theoretical model at one conference. Subsequently, a second conference paper described the primary experimental methodology that I used and the results, a third paper compared and contrasted the theory with the experimental data, and a fourth paper was prepared (but never submitted) describing the secondary experimental results over temperature. There were several common paragraphs in each paper, as they were discussing the same project and the background was identical. However, the work and results presented in each paper was different from each of the others, but each carried the same theme. ∎

VIGNETTE

Please Continue; It Would Not Make Any Difference

M. M. Tehrani, PhD, The Aerospace Corporation

One of the first rules of giving a conference talk is not to put too much information, in particular, too many equations on one chart. I was giving a talk at the annual meeting of the Optical Society of America in mid-1970. In those days, the presentation materials were produced on photo slides that were inserted into a slide projector. The speaker after me gave his slides to the person manning the projector and went to the podium. He started his talk entitled, "Solving the Double-Slit Diffraction Problem with Dirac Equations." He started reading from his written notes without looking at the screen. Except for his title slide, all of the presenter's slides were all filled with very lengthy equations and Dirac Operators in small letters. There was a noticeable hissing and humming among the audience. After he went through a large number of his slides, all the time concentrating on his notes, he looked at the screen and suddenly realized that his slides were upside down. He was terribly embarrassed especially since about 10 minutes of his 15-minute time had passed. He asked the person manning the projector if he could pull the rest of the slides out and turn them by 180 degrees. Someone from the audience yelled, "Please continue; it would not make any difference." ■

VIGNETTE

Appropriate References

Gale Mazur, EdD

At the urging of an instructor, I fine-tuned an application paper I had written as an assignment in a leadership course for a Society of Educators and Scholars (SES) conference and foolishly thought a little rewriting would transform the assignment into a publishable paper. My experience may offer a value lesson for students who want to use classroom assignments as a starting point for conference publications.

The application paper was a case study that described how a leader enrolled executives and built a team of peers to successfully accomplish a significant worldwide corporate initiative. I felt great when the abstract was accepted, and my presentation at the conference was well received. But I ran into trouble when the paper was peer-reviewed for a journal.

The journal's peer-reviewers liked the content and writing style of my paper, but they wouldn't accept the Northouse (2004) textbook that surveyed the literature on leadership as a reference source. Although it was acceptable as a class assignment to use the course textbook, the peer-reviewers would only accept articles as citations and references from peer-reviewed and scholarly sources. Publishing my case study required substituting all the secondary Northouse citations with valid primary sources. ■

VIGNETTE

Your Topic May Not Be What the Audience Is Interested in Hearing

Clare Berger, Author

At one conference, the authors presented a paper on organizational change at a private school. The authors approached it from a business perspective showing the analysis of organizational structure. However, the audience members were not business executives looking for a way to analyze their organizations but instead a group of high school principals who were more interested in how the private school was dealing with the issues in question. It took us by surprise, and the authors ended up fielding some difficult questions. If the authors had given more thought to focusing on the particular aspects this audience might be interested in, the authors would not have been caught off guard. Not all was lost. The authors learned from the experience and became better presenters because of it. Presenters need to know their audience and tailor their presentations to provide a clear value. ■

VIGNETTE

A Couple of Topics You Might Consider Covering

W. J. Riley, Hamilton Technical Services, www.wriley.com

The [*Writing for Conferences*] book sounds interesting and unique— I don't recall having ever seen one on that subject before. I don't have a story for you, just a few topics you might consider covering:

1. The biggest hassle is often getting approval for a paper from your management, customer, or the government. I can recall several instances

involving the GPS clock program where papers (mine and others) had to be withdrawn because of that. Organizations like Company X and Company Y are bad enough, but a program office is worse. No matter how early you start, it always comes down to the wire.

2. Always treat the written and oral presentations as two different things. You can't make a good oral presentation (or even poster presentation) by reading (or posting) the printed paper.

3. Always have the paper done before the conference (even if it is due afterward), and have preprints to give to people or e-mail to them.

4. A few years ago, at the Precise Time and Time Interval (PTTI) conference, there was an instance where a scheduled speaker from a well-known organization just didn't bother to show up. No phone call, no fax, no e-mail, no nothing. When the time came for him to make his presentation, he just wasn't there. This wasn't a case of no travel money, no visa, no paper approval, or even a sudden illness. He just wasn't there. When contacted soon afterward, no reasonable excuse was forthcoming. Now I'm sure no reader of your book would do something like that, but everyone should know that this is a serious breach of professional and ethical conduct that is never forgotten. ■

VIGNETTE

In the Days Before PowerPoint

Neal Brune, Vice President, Countermeasures R&D, Esterline Defense Group

I'm having trouble thinking back to my first conference paper. It had to have been more than 30 years ago. The tools and methods were much different then. People still used transparencies for slides, and they had to be made by some grumpy artist that lived in the basement and threw ink bottles at you if you made a change. For videos, you usually had a strip of 16 mm film that may have been carefully spliced by the scatterbrain that took pictures for the company. I loved the advent of PowerPoint because the authors could finally put the grumpy artist out to pasture. Only trouble is the artistic quality suffered greatly when I did it myself.

I guess the presentation butterflies lasted until I got to be chairman of my own conference; then I decided I couldn't use the hook on myself and had never used it on anyone else (even though I wanted to a couple of times), so life got better still.

One thing still remains: I volunteer to write papers too many times and say to myself, "Why do I do this when it's always a pain in the rear to get the thing ready, get it cleared, written, put up with co-authors, etc.?" As I sit writing this, I concluded that I need to go into the office tomorrow to work on my paper for October. My co-authors are taking this seriously. I was just going to get up and show a couple of slides and a few smoke-and-fire videos, prognosticate sagely about the future of the technology, and sit down. Now I have to have conference calls to fiddle with each slide and send CDs back and forth across the country. *Offer an abstract in haste, repent in leisure.*

Lastly; stand up, speak up, and shut up and sit down on time! ■

VIGNETTE

Practicing the Talk Over and Over

*Name withheld because she thought, "It's so **un**-profound!"*

I can't remember anything noteworthy about my first conference paper! The authors (my graduate advisor and I) submitted the paper, and it got accepted. I don't remember changing much based on review comments, if anything. I remember practicing the talk over and over, which really helped with the jitters. ■

VIGNETTE

I'd Like to Propose a Change in the Conference Format

Dr. David Silverberg, Assistant Professor, Dwight Schar College of Education, Ashland University, Ohio

"Does anyone want to present at a conference?" asked my statistics professor. The itch in my shoulder was more like a life-long craving in my gut, so I raised my hand. "The *Society of Educators and Scholars* conference is at the University of Texas this year, and, yes, Dave, you can apply to present."

I wrote my proposal, got accepted, and became immediately nervous about presenting in front of a group of academics. Three years later, I still remember that moment in Austin with my then-girlfriend, now wife, at my side. As the conference began, I prayed for a small and sleepy audience.

"I'd like to propose a change in the conference format," said my omnipresent statistics professor and event spokesperson. "Why don't the authors have the student-scholars present their work in front of the whole group, rather than in separate break-out student sessions?" In statistical terms, I experienced a profound and sudden regression in my critical region. He continued: "And I think Silverberg should start." Gulp.

It was as if all of Austin's 1.5 million Mexican free-tail bats, and celebrity local Willie Nelson, descended upon my puny doctoral ego. "OK." I smiled and proceeded to deliver my piece on the future of character education. What I remember most was my favorite professor's smile as I left the podium...and embarked on my career.

[Addendum from student (now Dr.) Leslie Evans who attended that conference: "I remember that moment and had the exact same reaction as I presented a few people after Dave. I had already practiced early that morning in a smaller breakout room."] ∎

VIGNETTE

Most People Lose Their Shirts in Las Vegas, but Mike Lost His Pants

Michael A. Moodian, EdD, Editor, Contemporary Leadership and Intercultural Competence (2008)

Among the numerous conferences that I have participated in, there is one that certainly stands out above all the others. The date was Saturday, March 24, 2007. A full morning was booked; first, I had press access to a presidential candidate forum sponsored by the Center for American Progress at the UNLV Cox Pavilion. While attending the forum, I was to step out for a 10:15 a.m. presentation at a conference (located across campus at the UNLV student union). The plan was to drive to Las Vegas from Southern California early in the morning, stop at the Mandalay Bay restroom to change into my suit (I always wear a t-shirt and shorts during long drives), and proceed to UNLV for the day's festivities.

At the time I was fresh off of a move to a new condominium, in the middle of writing my dissertation, and working on my first book— *Contemporary Leadership and Intercultural Competence.* Needless to say, my life was in disorder. I made it to Las Vegas in great time, pulled into the Mandalay Bay parking garage, and proceeded to the trunk of my car to retrieve my suit. The trunk popped open, I pulled the garment bag out, zipped it open to make sure that everything was there, and, to my surprise…I had forgotten to bring pants! Immediately, a pleasant morning drive had turned into a frantic mess. What was I going to do? The presidential candidate forum was in 40 minutes.

Holding a doctorate in the study of leadership, I did what any great leader would do in the face of adversity—I briskly walked into the Mandalay Bay looking for any clothing store that was open. It was early, so the pickings were slim. I found a Nike clothing store, charged in, grabbed the only pair of black pants that I could find, slapped my credit card on the counter, and proceeded to the dressing room as quickly as possible to change. There were two problems—for one, the pants were too long and they didn't offer my length; second, the cashier had no pins, so I grabbed a handful of paper clips, cuffed my new pair of pants, and ran out of the store.

I did end up making it to both events, including the talk with [then] Senator Barack Obama. The pants never did quite work out. They were black, so they seemed to match my suit as long as someone looked at me from 50 feet away. Plus, because they were too big, I had to continually pull them up or risk losing them. So my advice to any graduate student who is preparing for their first conference is to be prepared, remain calm, and please, by all means necessary, don't forget your pants. ■

VIGNETTE

I Might Have Broken Down and Cried

Ray M. Valadez, EdD, Practitioner Faculty of Economics, Pepperdine University, Graziadio School of Business and Management

Thank God my first conference paper was with co-authors that had some familiarity with the conference and had expertise on the topic. Otherwise, I might have broken down and cried! Partnering and sharing the moment is always a good way to start your publication and presentations. I was lucky in my first publishing attempt in that the graduate students I spent some time with were interested in publishing and had in fact written a paper in which I had advised them, and I was invited into the paper because of my expertise and experience with the subject matter. However, this made me no less nervous or apprehensive about the process. I did contribute to the effectiveness of the paper. In the end, I did spend a lot of time and energy but was happy with the outcome. ∎

VIGNETTE

There Is No Substitute for Good Conference Preparation

Stacey Hills, Assistant Professor of Marketing, Utah State University

I was very lucky to have an amazing first conference presentation, thanks largely to my dissertation advisor. It was an American Management Association Educator's Conference (no pressure, right?) and I was going to present work that was co-authored with two of my faculty. It wasn't my dissertation, but there was definitely pressure to represent my professors and my university well.

Wanting to be sure that I did a good job, my advisor reviewed my presentation (good old PowerPoint) about a week in advance and made sure that I had backups ready. He then did something that has stuck with me ever since—he made me write out my entire presentation! I'm normally a wing it sort of person, so this was tough. I wrote out transitions, ice breakers, you name it. He also had me prepare the answers to the most common questions that I was going to be asked.

I trusted him, and did what he asked. The presentation went really great, and those common questions were all asked! At the end of my session, the chair announced that this was my first conference and ceremoniously awarded me the transparency slide that introduced the session.

There is no substitute for good conference prep. ■

VIGNETTE

Engage the Audience

Michele A. Webb, Engineering Project Manager and Doctoral Student

Attending conferences and observing the participants reduced my stress when I began preparing my first conference paper and presentation. I found that the best conference papers/presentations were succinct and targeted for the audience, with illustrated examples and visuals (e.g., workflow diagrams to explain the framework). The best presenters were those who were able to engage the audience through storytelling, testimonies, interesting facts, and use of good public-speaking skills. Above all, I found that professional but natural humor is a great way to connect with the audience. ■

VIGNETTE

If You Enjoy Something You Must Either Be Good at It, or You Will Become Good at It

Vahid R. Riasati, PhD

I have never had any problem with public speaking; in fact, I generally enjoy it. Some say if you enjoy something you must either be good at it, or you will be good at it. I feel that it is also true that if you are afraid of something and are at the same time stubborn at facing your fear, you will be good at facing your fears. Often, successful speakers are non-paradoxical fear-fighters who enjoy smooth and tempered points of alternative viewing of topics that are linked by consideration; a lack of which does not lead to a fault. Being good at avoiding an issue is just as effective in speaking as knowing the topic one discusses. Well, here is my anecdote.

The first time I spoke was in my American history class with my fiery-red–headed teacher, Mrs. Summers. I gave my candid opinion about a topic that related to the discussion of freedom of speech; she paid attention to me because, at the time, Iran had taken some hostages, and I was the only Iranian in the 1,400-student high school. Because our discussion took the entire period, my friends asked me to speak more often. I indulged them, and Mrs. Summers and I talked about related topics every time our class met. From time to time, someone else would talk for about a minute or so, and this led to one of the few American history classes that kept its students awake, so said my classmates. I gave other presentations and enjoyed them all. Often, I had something to say, something that I thought was worth talking about, something that I wanted others to hear. I guess I would say that after all these years of speaking in public and teaching over six thousand students, if there were one thing worth learning it would have to be that people have a common soul and it craves others that care for it; give it that and you will always be a great speaker. ■

VIGNETTE

The Austin Manifesto

Chaz Austin, EdD, Pepperdine University MBA Career Counselor and Organizational Leadership Doctoral Student

I'd been teaching and writing articles on the subject of my first conference paper at various colleges for a number of years, so I knew the subject matter very well. The paper I wrote allowed me to put all the knowledge I'd gained over the years into one large document, a manifesto of my philosophy on the issue (like *The Communist Manifesto,* but without the communist part). If you continue to teach the same course over and over again and always seek to improve it, it's amazing how much information you collect over the years. My paper was an opportunity to write everything I'd learned up until then. It clocked in at 27 pages. As satisfied as I was with the final result, after I sent it to friends and colleagues for review, I was amazed at how much I'd omitted—or hadn't even thought of. I'm including those changes in the next iteration of the paper, which will be submitted to another conference. ∎

These vignettes, and others throughout this book, have given the readers a view into the experiences of some new and veteran authors about their early experiences with publishing at conferences.

Summary

As you can see from this chapter, there are many ways to generate a conference paper. You most likely already have some sources in your arsenal. As described by the authors, strategies for creating a conference submission can range from reworking an existing (high quality) class assignment to salami slicing a larger research report into two or three papers. Creating a conference paper can be fun and provide an opportunity to collaborate with a new colleague and can be a competitive advantage to set you apart from others in your field.

Bibliography

Berger, Clare, Leslie Evans, Leo Mallette, and Atit Suwandee. "Organizational Analysis Tools to Identify Cause and Corrective Action for Lack of Collaboration Between Principals in a Private School." Hawaii International Conference on Education, January 2005.

Clapham, Phil. "Publish or Perish." *Bioscience* 55 (5) (2005): 390–391.

Evans, Leslie. "Connecting the Global Learning Communities." Paper presented at the Annual Conference of the Society of Educators and Scholars, Austin, Texas, 2004.

Mallette, Leo. "Theory Pi—Engineering Leadership: Not Your Theory X, Y or Z Leaders." Paper presented at the IEEE Aerospace Conference, Big Sky, Montana, 2005.

Northouse, Peter G. *Leadership: Theory and Practice.* 3rd edition. Thousand Oaks, CA: Sage Publications, 2004.

Section IV

The Paper, Presentation, and Networking

The chapters in Section III reviewed who could help you write the paper, took you through the first step of writing and submitting the abstract, and identified the genesis of some papers. Now that your abstract has been accepted, this section walks you through the paper writing and presentation phases of your journey into the publishing landscape.

11. How Do I Write, and What Is Scholarly Writing?

12. How Do I Prepare for the Presentation?

13. Giving the Presentation

14. What Else Can I Do at a Conference?

15. How to Be the Best Session Chair

The first step (Chapter 11) is writing the paper and writing it in a scholarly way. The next step (Chapter 12) prepares you for the actual presentation, which is much different from the paper because it is more visually oriented, focuses on the results you found, and demonstrates how it ties in with the literature. Chapter 13 discusses the physical presentation at the conference, from the author's breakfast to the applause. Chapter 14 discusses other things to do at a conference. Chapter 15 talks about being a session chair. Let's get started by learning about the scholarly writing process.

Finally it comes down to writing the actual paper. (iStockphoto.com)

11

Writing Your Paper (in a Scholarly Way)

Academic writing is understood as a contribution to an ongoing intellectual dialogue. (Bucholtz 2010)

Introduction
OK, now that your paper has been accepted, what are the next steps? Yes, you are now obligated to write and present your paper. It's time to write.

Why Do I Need an Outline?
An outline is not always required for a conference paper, but experienced writers use outlines, and beginners use outlines for their papers. An outline is useful for organizing thoughts, gauging paper length, and managing the page count. Chapter 9 stated many authors simply start with an outline of what they want to talk about related to their topic. Most outlines have the following framework:

- Title block
- Abstract
- Introduction
- Body of paper: topics 1 to 3 (or more)
- Conclusions
- References

What Goes in the Paper?

This isn't rocket science, and there are hundreds of books on writing. Find one you like and use it. You can also read journals to get a feel for solid scholarly writing, or ask one of your professors for a good recommendation. Most likely, you already have written numerous scholarly papers during your educational journey to date.

This chapter is not meant as a substitute for a good book on composition of scientific articles. See if the following portions of a typical paper outline fit into the scheme of your paper and the requirements (if any) of the conference.

Title Block

The title, author names, their affiliation, and sometimes an address belong here. The information is generally centered. Author order is important. The protocol for listing authors varies by discipline and by journal if there is more than one author. Many articles have been written on this subject as well as in Chapters 8 and 9 of this book. Listing the authors in alphabetical order by last name is a common method of listing multiple authors. Another method is to list the authors in the order that they contributed to the research that is being published. It is also quite common for the author that is presenting the paper at the conference to be listed first, regardless of contribution to the paper. Listing the presenting author first makes it easier for the audience to associate the name of the author in the program with the person who is presenting at the front of the room.

Abstract

This abstract should be the same as the abstract you submitted to the conference. The only exceptions would be either corrections, clarifications, or the addition of more results since the original abstract was submitted. The abstract should include the key findings of your research.

Table of Contents

A table of contents is a nice addition if it is required by the conference. Otherwise, it adds very little that is not discussed in the introduction.

Introduction

The background, overview, and general literature review of your topic are presented here. This should be a quarter or a third of your total paper.

Body of Paper

This section may include parts of the literature review that were not discussed in the introduction. The methods should be stated, as should the limitations of the study. The results of the investigation should be a prominent part of the body, and the implications of the results should be discussed. Recommendations could be included here or, if they are short, in the conclusions.

Acknowledgments

Thank the people and institutions that helped you. They will appreciate it, and it gives you an opportunity to express your gratitude in writing.

Conclusion or Summary

This section should be short. It could be similar to the abstract but with less background and more results.

References

Place these after the conclusion.

Appendices

Place these after the references.

Biography

A short 100- to 150-word biography oriented to the conference in which you are presenting is sometimes allowed, sometimes prohibited, and sometimes required. The position of the biography is at the discretion of the conference. Some conferences require it before the abstract, whereas others place it after the references. If the instructions are silent about placement of the biography, the authors recommend placing the biography immediately following the conclusions (and before the references) or as the very last item (after the references and appendices). You can include a picture in conference proceedings that are published electronically if allowed and you are comfortable doing so.

Examples of biographies from the authors are shown in the next few paragraphs. The authors feel it is best to have several versions of your biography. There can be a full version that is appropriate where there is no page limit and shorter *specialized* versions for other applications. The authors say "specialized" because there are different areas of your personal and professional life that you may not need (or want) to share with a particular journal or if you want to emphasize, or brand, only one particular aspect of your career.

Example 1. A 255-word biography for Leo Mallette:

Dr. Leo Mallette provides technical and programmatic support at The Aerospace Corporation. Previously, he worked in project management of satellite systems at the Boeing Company for 30 years. He received BS and MS degrees in electrical engineering from the University of Central Florida and MBA and EdD degrees (in organizational leadership) from Pepperdine University. Dr. Mallette has published over 60 conference and peer-reviewed journal articles on atomic frequency standards, satellite systems, ground stations, optical detectors, root-cause investigation, genealogy, organizational ethics, publishing, and pruning trees. He is co-author of the book *Writing for Conferences* (Greenwood, 2011), co-editor of *The SPELIT Power Matrix* (CreateSpace, 2007), and author of *Images of America: Rancho Mirage* (Arcadia Publishing, 2011). His dissertation topic was *Publishing Rates of Graduated Education PhD and EdD Students* and was a member of a panel on *Getting Published: A Panel of Emerging Scholars*, at the 2006 AERA Annual Meeting. Dr. Mallette is a supporting business faculty at Pepperdine University and the University of Phoenix's doctoral program, and was an Instructor of Engineering at the University of Central Florida. Leo is a member of the Board of Visitors for Pepperdine University, a senior member of the Institute of Electrical and Electronics Engineers, a member of the advisory board for the Precise Time and Time Interval Conference, and a board member of the Society of Educators and Scholars. He and his wife Kathy live in Irvine and Rancho Mirage, California. They have one daughter and two granddaughters. He enjoys playing with his granddaughters, gardening projects, traveling, and writing.

Above, Leo is emphasizing his technical project management skills over a long period of time, education, publishing history, volunteer work, and adds a few words about his personal life. Specialized versions of this biography could: (1) add the number of years of membership with the IEEE; (2) delete the personal life section; (3) emphasize the engineering background over the education experience (or vice versa); and (4) the dissertation title may be eliminated if it does not positively contribute to clarifying Leo's brand to the intended audience.

Example 2. A 62-word biography for Clare Berger:

Clare Berger is an administrator in higher education, specializing in the area of communications. She received a Bachelor's Degree from the University of California, Irvine, a master's degree in business administration from Pepperdine University, and is currently working on a doctorate in organizational leadership at Pepperdine University. Her passion lies in education, with a purpose of helping students achieve their educational goals.

As you can see, Clare's bio is less detailed and focused on her passion for education. Either biography can work; it depends on conference requirements, intended audience and purpose, and in some cases, how comfortable you are in releasing personal information about yourself to others. Don't include anything you or your loved ones would not be comfortable seeing on national news or on the Internet.

In this section, the authors have discussed most parts of the paper from the title to biography. Once you have finished the work, it's always worthwhile to ask someone you respect and trust to review it.

What Is Scholarly Writing?

Jessica Clark and Kristen Murray, authors of *Scholarly Writing: Ideas, Examples, and Execution* (2010, 3–4), describe scholarly writing as a process of constructing papers in specialized topics using research conducted by experts. It's highly likely that you have been writing papers for quite some time while pursuing your educational goals, and many of those papers have been scholarly papers. Your conference paper should be a scholarly paper that is prepared with the intent of being published in a conference or journal and not a popular tabloid magazine.

Chapters 8, 9, and 10 discussed the early stages of the writing process, including ways to generate a conference paper, writing the abstract,
and determining whether to solo-author or co-author a conference paper.
Moving forward in the process, you will be reading and reviewing literature related to your paper topic, working with references, organizing your
paper on your own or with others, and finalizing your paper for successful
publication at the conference.

Literature Review

You will spend a significant amount of time focused on critically reading
and reviewing the research supporting your paper. Choose credible sources
from scholarly journals and books written by experts in your topic field.
It's easy to stray or cross into other topics and suddenly find yourself writing off topic or out of scope. Hopefully, your co-author(s) will be actively
engaged in the writing process and provide valuable feedback. If writing
solo, again, have someone you trust and respect review your work and continually ask yourself, "Is this necessary to the purpose of my paper?"

References

You must properly cite references in your paper, or you will be accused of
plagiarism, risking both your paper publication and your credibility. There
are numerous writing style books and citation guides (e.g., APA, MLA,
Chicago Manual of Style, etc.) available for purchase and on the Internet to assist you in appropriately citing references and that will help you
understand and avoid plagiarism. Often, your educational institution will
have plagiarism software available that you can use to check your paper; if
not, you can purchase plagiarism software for your computer.

Working with Others

The authors strongly suggest you collaboratively determine author roles
and responsibilities prior to writing your paper. It is often helpful to assign
responsibilities based on authors' strengths. For example, if you have an
author who enjoys researching and reviewing literature, have that author
focus on the literature review. Another author may be strong in writing and
creating a document that flows well or may be better at preparing charts
and figures. All authors should be involved in editing the document and

providing feedback in a professional and constructive manner. Negative and demeaning co-author behavior should not be tolerated.

Finalizing Your Paper

Again, all authors have a responsibility to review and proofread the final paper prior to submission unless other arrangements were agreed upon by the authors. Each author brings different areas of expertise and experience to the table, and as a result, provides unique and valuable feedback that contributes to producing a richer paper for your conference readers.

Additional outstanding scholarly writing articles you may find helpful during your writing process that are readily available in most university libraries. Two excellent articles are "New Domains: Navigating the World of Academic Writing" by Gould, Katzmarek, and Shaw (2007) and "Writing for Publication: Steps to Excellence" by Henson (2007).

Summary

In this chapter, it was recommended you use an outline for your paper, and general outline areas were covered. The authors then described what typically belongs in a conference paper and provided some biographies you can use as examples to brand yourself. The chapter ended with a section on scholarly writing. Although you may be or have been writing scholarly papers while pursuing your educational goals, it is important to remember to use the same standards of writing in your conference papers.

Bibliography

Bucholtz, Mary. "Tips for Academic Publishing," http://www.linguistics. ucsb.edu/faculty/bucholtz/sociocultural/publishingtips.html (cited August 1, 2010).

Clark, Jessica, and Kristen Murray. *Scholarly Writing: Ideas, Examples, and Execution.* Durham: Carolina Academic Press, 2010.

Gould, J. Christine, JoAnne Katzmarek, and Patricia Shaw. "New Domains: Navigating the World of Academic Writing." *Phi Delta Kappan* 88 (10) (2007): 776–780.

Henson, Kenneth. "Writing for Publication: Steps to Excellence." *Phi Delta Kappan* 88 (10) (2007): 781–786.

Preparation and practice take much of the anxiety out of presentations. (iStockphoto.com)

12

Preparing for the Presentation

Always treat the written and oral presentations as two different things.
You can't make a good oral presentation by reading the printed paper.
(W. J. Riley, personal communication, 2005)

Introduction

Chapter 9 discussed abstract preparation, and Chapter 11 reviewed writing the paper. This chapter will discuss presentation preparation you need to do *before* the conference, and Chapter 13 will discuss preparing for the presentation *at* the conference.

Preparing for your presentation is critical to your success at a conference. The more you are willing to practice prior to presenting, the better you will perform. Regardless what form your presentation takes—oral presentation, panel discussion, workshop, poster session, or table discussion—allowing ample time to prepare and practice ensures you are meeting conference requirements and gain the respect of conference participants. By following this chapter's simple preparation guidelines, you will be well prepared, well dressed, well groomed, and your audience will love you for it.

Thinking About the Presentation

Preparing for a presentation can be daunting to individuals, even those who have presented at conferences many times; it can especially daunting if you have never presented at a conference. If you fall into the *never presented* category, remember, you are not the only one; many individuals at conferences will experience feelings of nervousness, self-doubt, or stage fright. Fortunately, the authors have never witnessed any presenters passing out, so that's one fear you can dismiss immediately. At every conference you attend, you will find a multitude of individuals presenting for the very first time. Others have presented only once or twice whereas others are pros that you can observe, but even professionals can get nervous. This is your opportunity to experience, learn, and grow. Whether or not you are a gifted public speaker, a key element of an excellent presentation is allowing a generous amount of preparation time for your presentation. Here are some other hints.

Read Conference Literature

First, make sure you have read the conference literature, browsed the conference web site to familiarize yourself with the conference, and noted any requirements (e.g., such as bringing your own laptop or extension cords, how long can you present, etc.). Many conference Web sites post past conference proceedings that allow you to explore what level and types of papers are being accepted and presented. Upon arriving at the conference, you should also attend some of the sessions prior to your own presentation to get a feel for presentation styles and the environment's atmosphere (more on this in Chapter 13).

The authors have been embarrassed by simple things like bringing transparency-viewgraphs and not having access to an overhead projector, or, vice versa, bringing a beautiful multicolor presentation with animation on a CD-ROM or flash drive and not having a computer or projector in the room.

How Will You Present?

Second, you need to decide how you will present. Do you favor oral presentations with slides, or do you prefer to just speak? Do you plan to do a poster session or discuss a topic as part of a panel? These different

| The authors have never witnessed any presenters passing out. |

presentation venues are discussed in the next section. Many presenters use Microsoft's PowerPoint presentation program to communicate with their audience. Videos or 35 mm slides or transparencies can also be used. Transparencies are almost obsolete. They are cumbersome when having to change each transparency, but they have advantages of being able to write on them or put two on top of each other to compare data. Some presenters just stand and speak. The strategy to use *standing and speaking* can depend on how much time you have and how comfortable you are with speaking. If you have 20 to 30 minutes to present, the authors would recommend you use some other form of presentation to engage your audience. Videos to augment your discussion are usually worth the extra effort. It will be very difficult for you to keep the audience's attention for 30 minutes if you stand and talk in a monotone, or only have 3 slides, or have 103 slides. First, let's discuss the different types of presentation venues.

Types of Presentations

The different types of presentations (oral, panel discussion, workshops, poster sessions, and table discussions) are discussed in this section. Additionally, there are other methods of conveying information such as musical or singing performances, videos, debates, photo montages, and so on. These are not discussed in this book, but there may be a place for these in some conferences—for example: a photo montage would be very appropriate for a 50-year historical review of a professional society.

Oral Presentations

You should decide if you will lecture with or without visual aids. Oral presentations are the most common method for presenting information and are usually done with a computer and projector. They are rarely done with transparencies and an overhead projector. The overhead projector is becoming less and less used as the years pass. However, there are advantages to having transparencies: you can write on them and overlay two of them easily to compare data.

Some of the tips to remember about an oral presentation are to stand up (don't sit), speak loudly, don't read the slides, maintain eye contact with your audience, and vary the tone and tempo of your voice.

> Be sure to differentiate between your opinion and proven fact.

Poster Sessions

The second most common type of presentation style is the poster session. This is a wonderful way for first timers to break into the world of conferences because you have direct one-to-one interaction with the conference participants. An added benefit is that you are not required to prepare and present to a larger audience. Poster sessions are often held in a large conference room or a hallway that is simultaneously shared by all poster session participants. As a poster session participant, you are responsible to prepare and display a storyboard of your paper. Your storyboard is displayed on a table or a cork/magnetic board for a set period of time assigned by the conference. The duration is usually two hours. You are usually standing by your storyboard during that designated time period.

The format of your display in the poster session will not be a copy of your paper because only one person will be able to read it. The format should be large enough so that several people can read it simultaneously. These could be copies of a PowerPoint presentation or a large (4.5 feet) display that is shipped rolled up in a tube.

During the poster session, conference attendees will walk through the conference room, browse through various poster sessions of interest, and stop and chat with poster session authors to discuss their storyboard, ask questions, or request additional information. Be prepared to provide handouts or information for conference attendees interested in your work. You can hand out the information personally or leave it on the table for attendees to help themselves.

You can request to be placed in a poster session. You may hope to be accepted for a presentation, but if you do not meet conference paper submittal deadlines, or your paper does not fit into a conference category, conference coordinators may automatically place you into a poster session. Do not be discouraged if you end up in a poster session against your desire. Poster sessions are an excellent way to network, build relationships, obtain new information, and discuss your work with individuals sharing similar interests.

This is the time to develop your presentation with various durations. You need the 5- to 10-second version (the elevator speech) to capture the interest

> Before anything else, preparation is the key to success.
>
> Alexander Graham Bell (1847–1922)

of the people who are strolling through the poster session area. If they are interested, they will stop and read your slides or ask you questions. If they aren't interested, you've only wasted 10 seconds of talking (this can add up after two hours). You'll need the one-minute speech for each major section of your paper. Some readers will be more interested in your methods, or your test technique, or your population, and some may even be interested in your results. Some may see the school name in your affiliation and have no interest in your paper, but may be an alumnus and ask you if Dr. Bob is still teaching there. Some of these discussions may be your first informal job interview with Company X! You should also be prepared to go into excruciating detail with the few interested people who are in your field. Conversely, be prepared to stand around with nothing to do if no one is interested in your topic. Do not leave your poster session until the designated time.

Panel Discussions

A panel discussion is also a form of presentation that typically lasts for 60 to 90 minutes to allow the assigned three to five panelists to make introductory remarks, state their position, be asked questions, and generate discussion. There are generally four to seven panelists with differing viewpoints and a panel moderator. The panelists' views are sometimes diametrically opposite and this makes for interesting and often entertaining discussions. The panel moderator introduces the topic, the panelists, calls on the panelists, and takes questions from the audience. The moderator is often an expert and will ask piercing and insightful questions.

Panel discussions require you to know your material thoroughly so you can respond to questions. If you are a first timer, it is likely you will not be asked to participate in a panel discussion setting. However, if the conference is small, or if it's a student panel, there is a good possibility it could happen. If so, embrace it as a learning experience and an opportunity to grow.

The authors have participated in many panel sessions where some questions are expected or *seeded,* and the participants are able to prepare answers ahead of time. If you are an expert in your field, you've probably heard variations of the same questions at work or in your classrooms. The questions are asked initially by the panel moderator, sometimes by other panelists as the different viewpoints are aired, and many questions come from the audience. The questions can be quite direct and controversial. Be sure to differentiate between your opinion and proven fact.

Workshops

Workshops are typically interactive, and work is done as a group or in small teams as opposed to listening to a presentation. Workshop presenters have group materials prepared ahead of time and guide the group or teams through exercises. Workshops often close with a sharing of results, followed by general discussion. Again, if you are a first timer, it is unlikely you will be appointed as a workshop presenter. If appointed, you will be notified through e-mail, on the Web site, or by letter that you are expected to hold a workshop. If you have an opportunity to participate in a workshop, doing so will prepare you for your future as a workshop presenter.

An example of a workshop presented by the authors (and this should not surprise you) was on the topic of getting published. The publishing landscape was introduced and handouts were passed out. The handouts looked like the *preparing an abstract* thought-experiment in Chapter 10. Small teams of two or three people were formed to brainstorm a publishing idea from each participant. The participants were asked to visualize an interesting part of their lives, to complete a few open-ended statements, and share within their small teams about how their answers formed the basis for an abstract. Each participant shared the results with the larger group and generated immense enthusiasm, insights, camaraderie, and potential for teaming once people learned that others in the workshop had similar interests.

Table Discussions

Several round tables seating 10 to 12 people will be set up in a large hall. There can be as many as 20 tables in a single room. One author is assigned to each table. The author arrives and verbally presents the topic to the attendees sitting at the table. There may be a small number of handouts given to the participants. This is intended to be an intimate two-way discussion with

> *Never* stand and *read* your paper or slides.

the author and would be more in depth than a poster session. Since everyone is sitting down, it is also more comfortable and longer-lasting than a poster session conversation. The duration of the table discussion is usually 45 minutes: longer than the oral presentations and shorter than the poster session.

This section prepared you for the type of presentation that you will do. The next section discusses the slides you may use—usually for oral sessions.

Preparing Your Slides
Allow plenty of time to prepare your presentation. Designing your slides and templates can be quite time consuming. The authors have provided a list in Appendix 12A that you can refer to for help in developing your presentation. You can also find friends or fellow students that are familiar with various presentation styles to assist you. Get feedback from people you trust. Work on your presentation, step away from it for a day or two, and go back to it refreshed and clear minded. You will notice things you did not notice before. An old rule of thumb is to allow 3 minutes per slide. You know your material and you may need only eight slides in 20 minutes, or you may have simple pictures and be able to flip through eight slides in a minute. If you have a 20-minute presentation, you should plan to have no more than a dozen slides (including your title page).

Preparing Your Words
Once you have prepared your slides, you can start practicing the words you will use with each slide. The words have to match but augment the slides. Also, *never* stand and *read* your paper or slides. This is taboo for a conference (and for almost any other presentation). Not only is reading your paper out loud considered unprofessional, it is rude, makes you look unprepared, and will put your audience to sleep. If the slides do not support what you want to say, then you need to change the slides or your words.

Once you've decided on the words and have the slides aligned with the words, you are ready to practice the talk. Make sure you time yourself and don't under-run your time by too much and certainly don't overrun your time. You never want to overrun your presentation and not get to your conclusions, so allow yourself time to conclude. Again, preparation and practice will prevent these things from ever happening to you.

Begin with a Roadmap

Always begin your presentation with an agenda that acts as a road map to guide the audience on this journey. The authors recommend Microsoft PowerPoint as a professional aid, and it seems to be universally available. A road map lets the audience know what to expect, allows them to follow the progression of ideas, and track the time. The attendees have less anxiety when they can see light at the end of the tunnel. An agenda will tell the audience in broad terms what you plan to share with them and may eliminate premature questions. The format is often as follows:

- Introduction (tell them what you will tell them)
- Background, methodology, results, discussion (tell them)
- Conclusions (tell them what you told them)

You will not need to announce to the audience the length of time you intend to take for your presentation—it is usually in the program. Managing that time properly shows that you value the audience's time and use it wisely. Figure 12.1 is an example of an agenda for a presentation.

Practice, Practice, Practice

Practice, practice, practice! Give your presentation to your spouse, significant other, coworker, one of the neighbors, or even your dog. Your cat probably won't listen, but your dog will, especially if you learn to insert

---

Audiences typically do not appreciate presenters going over the time limit.

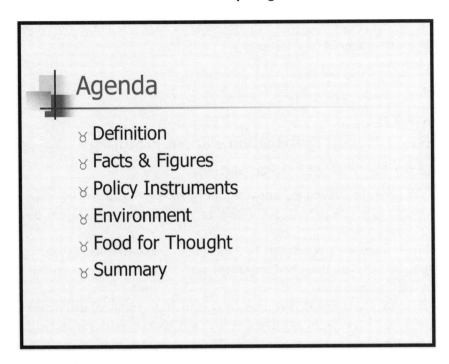

Figure 12.1.
PowerPoint Slide Showing an Agenda

changes of tone in your voice. You may want to record (audio or video) and critique yourself. Be sure to pace your presentation to stay within the time parameters. Conference organizers and audiences typically do not appreciate presenters going over the time limit. It is discourteous to the next presenter, and your session chair may stop your presentation if you go over the time limit. Conferences will have a *session chair* to monitor time. Session chairs have authority over the session and will direct presenters accordingly (see Chapter 15). The session chair may choose to signal you when you have five minutes left, but if you are going over your time allotment, the session chair may signal you to end your presentation. Frequently, when there are parallel sessions, audience members may get up and leave while you are talking because they need to get to another session down the hall. Be sure to talk with your session chair before the session, understand that you will present for a fixed amount of time, and allow a few minutes for questions.

I Never Made a Presentation without Practicing

G. Edward Bryan, Pacific Palisades, California

In 1967, for the Fall Joint Computer Conference, I was to give a presentation covering my paper. I didn't think there would be any problem, but how wrong I was!

In those days the powers that ran the FJCC knew what was needed to get a good presentation, and they made authors work to get it—at least first-time presenters.

First they sent me to a course on presentation graphical techniques. The teacher was from Hughes Aircraft, and his business was to teach engineers what should (or should not) be in a presentation. All the rules were there about size of font that would be readable in the back of a room, how many bullets to put on a slide, how not to clutter the presentation slides with all the detail of the paper, but just to stick to the important stuff—but it is *all* important, and I am so proud of it all.

But that was just the beginning. They made me practice. I was required to stand up in front of the evaluation team and give my talk as it would be given to the eventual audience—several hundred—as this was the biggest computer conference of the era.

Boy, was I terrible the first time: uncertain about what I should say, or how to say it and how to get all my material into the allotted time. I was required to practice again and again until it all worked. I can't remember how many times it took, but the lesson was there, not just for this FJCC, but for all time. I continue to be amazed at the patience and dedication of the evaluation team.

Always after, I never made a presentation without practice, even if it was just for me.

This was one of the best lessons I ever learned; it was valuable throughout my career. ∎

Feedback

Every good presentation needs feedback. The authors recommend you get it before the conference presentation, when you have time to make corrections. Seek out forums for practice runs. This could be at school, in front of your family, or for your work colleagues. Do not just present to yes-men and yes-women. You need critical feedback and not just, "Oh, yeah, that was great." Feedback provides you with valuable information you may use going forward that could improve your presentation skills, discover information your audience enjoyed and would like more of, or delete information where necessary.

The Power of Stories

You need to tell the conference audience what you have come to communicate. Many feel that the most powerful way to communicate is with stories. Stories remain in people's minds long after the facts have disappeared from memory. They will remember the emotions behind the story and the impression it made when you first told them. Stories help capture the audience and put them in the frame of mind to understand the results or implications of your presentation. There are many styles of storytelling, including a funny opening joke, describing a moving experience, telling about a business experience that your audience can relate to, or describing a current event that links to your discussion. Whatever your style may be, it helps to get practice in the art of storytelling. One proven way to do this is to join a Toastmasters International club and work on the different ways to capture the attention of your audience. There are many books that give presentation guidance, but there is no substitute for actual practice. Seize every opportunity to tell your stories to whomever will listen. Examples of storytelling are the vignettes sprinkled throughout this book, and the stories about misreading the audience of high school principals and the 45- to 20-minute shortened time slot in earlier sections of this chapter. In

---

Proper grooming and hygiene are expected and cannot be taken for granted.

storytelling, practice makes better, or least better than if you did not practice. More information about storytelling can be found in the book by John Walsh (2003), *The Art of Storytelling: Easy Steps to Presenting an Unforgettable Story.*

How Do I Look?

It's a good idea to *always* look like a professional at a conference. This section discusses what to wear, grooming, and hygiene.

What to Wear

You should *always* dress like a professional at a conference. Even if you are at a conference in Hawaii, think twice when you are tempted to throw on shorts, a Hawaiian shirt, and a pair of flip flops to present (OK, the Hawaiian shirt may be fine). There may be a travel conference in the Caribbean where shorts may be appropriate, but the authors have never been to one. Appearance is important because you are representing your school, your organization, and you are branding yourself. You want your audience to remember you for your work and not for your poor fashion sense. Consider spending money on a nice suit or business attire. Ladies often wear suits, but a tailored dress is considered professional as well. Denim jeans have become the de facto pants of choice for engineers and scientists in many laboratories. However, a conference is a forum for presenting laboratory data and is not an extension of your lab.

If you are presenting with a colleague, be sure to check with each other to ensure you are both wearing appropriate business attire. If you are budget challenged, see if you can borrow a sport coat or a suit just for the conference. You can also hint to people who love you (and are interested in your future) that you need a suit or jacket for your birthday. As a side note, if someone does buy a suit for you—please remember to send a thank you note with a picture of you wearing the suit. It would be best if the picture was taken at the conference. It is a nice touch to include a copy of your paper—they may not understand the contents, but they will show it to their family and friends.

Grooming and Hygiene

Proper grooming and hygiene are expected and cannot be taken for granted. However you wear your hair (short, long, shaved, or ponytail); get it taken care of before the conference. When you are at the conference, plan to use a bathroom, use deodorant, and brush your teeth before your presentation, especially if you will be close to people (as in a poster session). Check to make sure you are zipped, buttoned, and tied. And don't scratch any part of your body during your presentation. If it itches, live with it, or use the podium as a shield and be very discreet.

You want to be remembered as the person with a specific expertise and a professional manner—not the one with (1) the long hair who (annoyingly) kept brushing their bangs out of their field of view, (2) long nose hair, (3) the overly bushy eyebrows (yikes!), (4) broccoli in their teeth, (5) the dripped tomato ketchup in their beard or on their blouse, (6) excessive exposed chest (this applies to women and men), (7) excessive perfume or cologne, or (8) halitosis that would offend a moose. You may be smiling as you read this paragraph, but you've met people like this, and you don't want to be one of them. Check yourself in a mirror from a distance and close up. Trim or pluck those eyebrows and brush and floss and gargle—go to your room and brush your teeth after lunch if your presentation is in the afternoon. Proper grooming and hygiene are expected and cannot be taken for granted.

Summary

Whether you are presenting an oral presentation, poster session, table discussion, or in a panel discussion or workshop, you now know the secret to a successful presentation—preparation and practice. Your dress, grooming, and hygiene during a presentation were reviewed. To help you remember the guidelines discussed throughout this chapter, a checklist is provided on the following page to guide you through your preparation period. Now you are ready to present your paper. Be sure to have plenty of business cards. Conferences are a gold mine for networking (more in Chapter 14), and business cards are your connection to others that could lead to valuable relationships in the future.

Checklist to Prepare for Your Presentation

- Carefully read the conference literature ahead of time.
- Select your preferred presentation style.
  - Oral presentation
  - Panel discussion
  - Workshop
  - Poster session
  - Table discussions
- Prepare your presentation in the right format.
- *Never* stand and *read* your paper.
- Allow plenty of time to prepare your presentation and practice, practice, practice!
- Be prepared to cut back or lengthen your presentation as needed.
- *Always* dress like a professional at a conference.
- Proper grooming and hygiene are expected and cannot be taken for granted.
- Don't forget to bring plenty of business cards.

Bibliography

Walsh, John. *The Art of Storytelling: Easy Steps to Presenting an Unforgettable Story.* Chicago: Moody, 2003.

Appendix 12A

A List of Web Sites and Books for Help in Working on Your Presentation

Essential Communication Strategies: For Scientists, Engineers, and Technology Professionals, 2nd Edition, Herbert Hirsch, ISBN: 978-0-471-27317-2, 200 pages, December 2002, Wiley-IEEE Press

Purdue University's online writing lab (OWL), http://owl.english.purdue. edu/

The Short Road to Great Presentations: How to Reach Any Audience Through Focused Preparation, Inspired Delivery, and Smart Use of Technology, Cheryl Reimold and Peter Reimold, ISBN: 978-0-471-28136-8, 360 pages, June 2003, Wiley-IEEE Press

Toastmasters International Web site, http://www.toastmasters.org

Writing and Speaking in the Technology Professions: A Practical Guide, 2nd Edition, David F. Beer (Editor), ISBN: 978-0-471-44473-2, 517 pages, July 2003, Wiley-IEEE Press

Writing in the Technical Fields: A Step-by-Step Guide for Engineers, Scientists, and Technicians, Mike Markel, ISBN: 978-0-7803-1036-0, 296 pages, March 1994, Wiley-IEEE Press

After all the hard work of research, writing, planning, and practice comes the actual presentation. (iStockphoto.com)

13

Giving the Presentation

Stand up, speak up, and shut up and sit down on time! (Neal Brune, personal communication, 2007)

Introduction

Chapter 12 discussed the presentation preparation you need to do *before* the conference, and this chapter will discuss preparing for the presentation *at* the conference. One of the most critical parts of your conference experience will be giving the presentation, but there is no need to panic—remember that the audience wants you to succeed. By following the tried-and-true advice in Chapters 12 and 13, you will make it through the experience successfully and will enjoy yourself in the process. One of the greatest fears is speaking in public, but this can be overcome with preparation and attention to detail. To really sell the ideas you have written in your conference paper and to impress editors who may be considering your paper for inclusion into a journal, you will need to come across as

> Tell them what you are going to tell them.
> Tell them.
> Tell them what you told them.
>
> Old Adage

knowledgeable in the subject matter and passionate about the topic. Remember, the audience came to hear you speak because they are interested in your topic. They want to learn something from you, they want you to succeed, and the authors of this book want you to succeed.

The Presentation

It is essential to know your audience and to have a plan to effectively use their time. You must tell them what you will share with them, share the information, and then follow with a summary of the key points. To really connect with the audience and make a lasting impression, it is important to let your passion for the topic show through.

If at all possible, try a dry run in the actual conference presentation room—most conference rooms and their presentation equipment are open during lunch, session breaks, and the mornings before the conference sessions officially begin. Load your presentation and check for lighting, how well the visuals show up, and how the projector works. How loud do you need to be to be heard in the back of the crowded room with a couple of people carrying on a quiet side conversation?

Be Flexible

Finally, be prepared to cut back or lengthen your presentation as needed. There are times when the conference coordinators or the session chair might cut back your time due to a variety of reasons (i.e., combining

---

It is smart to have slightly shorter and longer versions of your presentation.

Definition

Parallel sessions are when two or more papers are being presented in two or more separate rooms at the same time.

sessions due to room or projector unavailability), whereas at other times, a presenter may not show up due to a missed flight, and you are given more time than originally planned. You can, of course, decline the extra time and just end your presentation accordingly. Some attendees are happy to end the session early because it allows them to ask questions, meet others, and network.

VIGNETTE

Flexibility

Leo Mallette, EdD

One example of flexibility was a 90-minute session in which three half-hour papers were to be presented. The authors of the first and third papers did show up prior to the session. Since there were parallel sessions, the session moderator did not allow the second paper to start early, but held an informal conversation with the audience about a subject that had broad general appeal. When it came time for the second paper to begin, and other conference attendees from other parallel sessions came into the room at the appropriate time, he introduced the second paper and kept the paper to its half-hour slot, but allowed questions and answers to continue into the slot for the third paper. This way, the session moderator was able to use the session time wisely with an ad-hoc discussion in the first paper's time slot, followed by the scheduled second paper, and a more in-depth discussion period in the third paper's time slot. ∎

Watch Your Timing

Starting your presentation on time and staying on time in your session is critical to the flow of the conference and respectful to the other presenters and the audience. If your session is scheduled for 20 minutes, it is smart to have a 15-, 20-, and 30-minute version of your presentation. Sometimes conferences will change the amount of allotted time at the last minute due to presenters not showing up, rearranging presenter's time slots, or condensing sessions (for example: if an earlier session exceeded their time allotment). Know which slides you can skip if you have to. Practice giving the different variations of your talk and have someone time you. Make sure to keep the most important concepts intact. The conference will usually reserve at least a small amount of time for questions or discussion at the end of your presentation.

At their first conference, one of the authors' friends was allotted a 45-minute time slot and had practiced her presentation well. On the actual day of the presentation, it was decided that two previously parallel sessions would be combined so that all attendees could hear all the presentations instead of having to choose between two sessions. This resulted in two presenters having to share the 45-minute time slot. The author had about 25 slides, timed perfectly (with time for audience participation) at about 45 minutes. Without any practice, she had to get up and deliver a 20-minute presentation and try to convey the same information. She was flying through slides, unsure of which to pass by. It was a harrowing experience, but now she knows that it is smart to plan ahead for just such an occasion.

Don't Read the Paper

Don't read the paper, don't read your slides, and don't read from note cards. Your paper may have sizable sections for the introduction, background, and methods. Your audience is attending your presentation to hear your results. So be brief with the introduction and background information. For example, you might say, "There are many papers on marsupials, but very few studies of the organizational leadership structure within kangaroo herds." This simple sentence orients the audience, dispenses with long review of what other studies have done, gives the problem statement, and leads the audience to ask the same research question you will be addressing in your presentation: How are kangaroo herds organized? However, there are exceptions. If your paper is a historical review paper or is describing a new method of online surveying, then you must spend your presentation time on these subjects because they are your results.

Visual Aids

Once you have captured the audience's attention, and they sit riveted to the edge of their seats in anticipation of your next words, it is time to give them the facts (the bulk of what your research found or the new theory you have created).

Slides. Visuals are important to keep their interest high. Make sure the visuals are easy to see from the back of the room and pertinent to your point. They should support what you are saying and not be a substitute for content. Keep your graphics simple. Less is definitely more. Let the eye pass in one sweep over the information. Avoid putting large amounts of text on your slides; bulleted short phrases, or plots instead of tables, are important on slides to prevent the audience from trying to read your slides instead of focusing on you and the point you are making. Keep font sizes and styles uniform to prevent distraction.

Handouts. Another form of visual aid is the handout. It may be wise to bring a few copies of your paper or slides for those who are really interested in it and don't want to wait to receive the proceedings. You might also consider bringing sufficient copies of your slides for the entire audience, so that attendees can take notes while you are presenting. Providing your e-mail address on the handouts will allow interested audience members to contact you at a future time to ask more questions or propose collaborations. Handouts can be printed with two or four slides per page, and copied double-sided, to save paper and weight. *Caveat:* Remember that the presenter is the focus of the presentation and not the slide presentation—the slides are there to augment your words and results.

Summarize

It is extremely important to wrap up your presentation by summarizing the key points you have made. This summary slide (and it should be a single

---

Reminder

The presenter, not the PowerPoint, is the focus of the presentation.

slide) should be your last slide. Leave it up on the screen while you take questions. Keep it brief and focus only on the main takeaways you want the audience to leave with. This is a good time to show how you linked each topic to the main point. By focusing on just three to five points, there is a better chance that the audience will leave with a clear memory of what you wanted to impart to them. They can always contact you for additional details

Let Your Passion Show

Enthusiasm is contagious. Let your audience see how much you care about your topic. As Marion Clare, renowned presentation coach says "Allow yourself to be wonderful" (personal communication, 2007). Make eye contact with your audience. This exudes confidence. Trust your content. You have worked hard to prepare a well researched paper, and the presentation is a way to share this exciting information with interested parties. Table 13.1 is a summary of some of the key points the authors have discussed.

Know Your Audience

Take active measures to find out who is in the audience and who will be presenting with you during your session. Check the conference program to see if your fellow session presenters are presenting during any other

---

TABLE 13.1
Checklist of Presentation Guidelines

- Know your audience (who is attending and what do they want?)
- Watch your timing
- Begin with a road map
- Use storytelling
- Use appropriate visual aids
- Summarize key points
- Let your passion show

sessions at the conference and take the time to go hear their other presentation. Introduce yourself ahead of time to audience members and fellow session presenters on an individual basis. Doing so will create an additional layer of comfort when it's your turn to present. One of the vignettes submitted for this book emphasized this topic.

VIGNETTE

Know Your Audience

Adam Abrahamzon

Unfortunately, I don't have any good stories I can include in your book. My only words of wisdom for those new to publishing or presenting at conferences are to understand the size and background of the potential audience.

Writers and presenters should take into account the expected number of readers or conference participants and their background. Presenting to 20 professors of related fields requires more detail than if the presentation were given to the same number of students in unrelated fields of study. Presenters must consider whether they are comfortable presenting to a live audience of 100 or a remote audience of 400. ■

Your presentation should start well before you approach the podium. The first step to knowing your audience (in addition to your contemplation of their interests while preparing your paper) is to attend several sessions before you are scheduled to speak and listen to the papers, the presenter's tone, the questions, and the presenters that are well received. The second step is to walk around the conference and greet your fellow attendees. Ask their names, shake their hands, and inquire where they are from. This way you will be speaking to new friends instead of strangers. It helps to calm the nerves to know you have a few things in common with some of them. Also, it gives you a sense of the audience's background and possible interest in your presentation.

VIGNETTE

We Misread the Audience

Clare Berger, Author

At one conference, the authors of this book presented a paper on the organizational change occurring at a private school. The authors approached it from a business perspective and showed an analysis of the school's organizational structure. It turned out the audience members were not business executives looking for a way to analyze their organizations but instead a group of high school principals who were more interested in how the private school was dealing with the issues in question. It took the authors by surprise, and they ended up fielding some difficult questions. If they had given more thought to focusing on the particular aspects this audience might be interested in, they would have been better prepared for the question and answer session. Not all was lost; they learned from the experience and became better presenters because of it. Presenters need to know their audience and tailor their presentations to provide a clear value. ■

Engaging the Audience

There are several techniques for speaking to an audience. They include changing the speed of your speaking, changing the tone of your talk, and using both visual and verbal stimulation. It often helps to poll the room and ask an easy question as it comes up in the discussion. This could be as simple as "I went to UCLA, how many of you did?" or "How many of you have ever petted a penguin?" This pulls in the audience, and you can

---

Definition: Discussant

A specific member of the audience who has read your paper beforehand and is prepared to comment on the paper and presentation immediately after the presentation.

continue your presentation with the key UCLA or penguin fact that you want them to remember. *Don't* use the hackneyed jest, "There will be a test on this at the awards banquet." Appendix 12A lists books on writing, speaking, and presenting, and the Toastmasters International Web site at http://www.toastmasters.org has many useful suggestions for speakers.

Discussants

Discussants are not part of every conference, but, when present, the discussant may be your most critical reviewer. She has read your paper and has been chosen because she is knowledgeable in the area you are discussing. Discussants are usually given three to five minutes following the presentation and before the Q&A session to critique your paper. They may critique the content of the paper, the content of the presentation, the style of writing, or your presentation style. The discussant's words may be kind or cutting.

One example of comments from your discussant might include praise such as:

- This paper was a very interesting read, was thoroughly researched, and I enjoyed the applicable stories told by the author.

  There may be comments regarding omissions such as:

- The paper was well supported by the popular theories, but I would have liked to have seen the author address the alternate views presented by Smith (1995) and Jones's (2003, 2005, and 2006) extensive research.

The poorly prepared paper is often met with unfavorable remarks from the discussant. If your paper was inadequately prepared, you may hear comments such as:

- This paper was poorly researched and did not address any of the previous studies in the field.
- The paper would benefit from an editor who was familiar with the language.

> **Prepare!**
>
> One poorly presented paper is worse than not having published.

- The results do not follow from, and actually contradict, the data presented in Table 1.
- The text indicates that Figure 3 summarizes the results, but that figure was not included in the paper.

You want to avoid comments like these by adequately preparing the paper and presentation. One poorly presented paper is worse than not having published.

Question and Answer Period

Fielding questions from the audience at the end of your presentation can be stressful. If not handled confidently, this can end your presentation on an unfavorable note. Look around; people will usually raise their hands; point at people to signal them to ask their question. If no one has any questions, look to your session chair—they may have a question (maybe even one that you suggested for them—see Chapter 15). If hands do go up, do not panic. You probably only have about five minutes of questions before the next presenter takes the stage. Answer a few questions, end your presentation with smile, and a "Thank you for your attention."

Tips. It helps to take questions from a variety of people—don't let a single audience member dominate the questioning if there appear to be multiple questions from the audience. Paraphrase the question for people in the audience who may not have heard the question. This helps the audience understand the question, and allows the one who asked the question be sure you understood the question. Be thorough, but do not give an extensive answer that takes up the entire time allotted. It is perfectly acceptable to indicate when you don't know the answer. Depending on the applicability to your topic, you can turn the question back to the audience or offer to look into it further. You can also point the questioner in the right direction to research the answer for himself. Never try to make

TABLE 13.2
Checklist for Questions and Answers

- Take questions from a variety of people
- Don't overlook the questions from people in the back of the room
- Paraphrase the question for the audience
- Be thorough, but do not give an extensive answer that takes up the entire time allotted
- It is perfectly acceptable to indicate that you don't know the answer
- Ask the audience for their opinions
- Offer to look into the issue further
- Point the questioner in the right direction to research the answer for himself
- Never try to make up an answer
- Be professional

up an answer. The authors have found most questioners to be genuinely interested in the topic and sincere in their request for additional knowledge. Most of all, watch your time. Do not intrude on the next presenter's time or extrapolate from your presentation or experience level. A checklist of ideas for the Q&A session is presented in Table 13.2.

Difficult Audiences. In the rare instances when problems occur, no matter how tempting it may be, do not return hostility. Keep calm. Hecklers or grandstanding can be deflected by asking, "And what was your question?" or with a simple "Thank you for your observation; are there any other questions?" or relying on the session chair to maintain control of the audience. You may want to review the "Problem Resolution" section in Chapter 15 for examples of problems that your session chair may encounter. Don't be one of your session chair's problems. Be professional at all times.

Tips for Cross-Cultural Communication

Wherever the conference is held, there will be attendees from various ethnic and geographical backgrounds. Listening to native speakers from Fargo, North Dakota; Savannah, Georgia; and Boston, Massachusetts may give you a taste of the vastly differing regional accents from only one country.

Be careful with colloquialisms, humor, idioms, local lingo, religion, sarcasm, slang, speaking quickly, and sports metaphors. A very short list of examples of poor and improved statements is given in Appendix 13A. Try to be prepared for unusual questions—even those that you have answered in your presentation—and be diplomatic and professional at all times.

Summary

Giving the presentation is one of the most critical parts of the conference experience. It does not need to be a stressful situation if you plan ahead and follow the guidelines set forth in Chapters 12 and 13. Your presentation is really an opportunity to sell the ideas you have written in your conference paper and to impress those who may be considering publishing it in other venues. You want to come across as knowledgeable in the subject matter and passionate about your topic. The audience wants you to be a successful presenter, because they want to come away with an appreciation and understanding of your material.

Appendix 13A

Examples of Good and Bad Usage

Colloquialisms

Original. We added pop to the mixture. (United States, Midwest)
> *Improved.* We added 50 milliliters of a carbonated soft drink to the mixture.

Original. We removed the test equipment from the boot. (British)

Original. We took the test equipment out of the trunk. (United States)
> *Improved.* We removed the test equipment from the vehicle.

Humor

Bad Humor. We all know that (pick a nationality) are not very (pick an attribute).

Better. I'm not one to talk—it took me five years to get my
bachelor's degree!

Bad Humor. Don't wander into the ballroom next door because they don't
want us there.

Better. Let's respect the people in the next room. We didn't
invite them to our conference, and they didn't invite us to
their wedding.

Idioms

Idiom. He kicked the bucket.

Idiom. He went to the big laboratory in the sky.

Idiom. He passed.

Clear Statement. He died.

Local Lingo

Lingo. The authors of this book are from the OC. (United States,
Southern California)

Correct. The authors of this book are from Orange County,
California.

Lingo. Then y'all add some…(Southern United States)

Correct. Next, you would add 100 milliliters of…

Example: A presentation (in this case a song) with a decidedly local
flavor is the beautiful song "Waltzing Matilda"—it is filled with
Australian lingo from the turn of the 20th century. Even the title is
filled with Australianisms: *Matilda* refers to the swag (what many of
us would call a bedroll or backpack) of a homeless person and *waltzing*
refers to his travels around Australia looking for work. The song's lyr-
ics are similarly written with Australian lingo.

Religion

Bad. I don't want to say anything bad about (*pick a religion*), but…

Good. (Silence)

Sarcasm

Original Statement. I didn't ask for much.

> *Truth.* This research was completed on time because everyone on the team worked many long hours and weekends.

Slang

Slang. The woofus output was at 10 gig. (acronyms and abbreviations)

> *Translation.* The output frequency of the wideband frequency synthesizer was nominally 10 gigahertz.

Slang. Hey. I see my homeys in the back. (United States, ethnic)

> *Translation.* Good morning. It's good to see people from my company and everyone else who is interested in my presentation on...

Speaking Quickly

Bad. On-this-slide-you-see-that-beta-is-less-than-twenty-and-on-this-next-slide...

> *Good.* This slide shows the variation of the transistor gain, beta, over the last two years. (*Pause.*) We can see here (*point with laser pointer*) that beta decreases below 20 dB. This shows that the test induced unacceptable degradation within about 22 months.

Sports Metaphors

Metaphor. Going for the gold. (Olympics)

> *Translation.* Trying very hard to win.

Metaphor. We just got to first base with two strikes against us. (baseball)

> *Translation.* We finally made quantifiable progress on this project after the two setbacks that almost depleted our reserve budget.

Metaphor. She hit a homerun. (baseball)

Metaphor. She ran a touchdown. (United States, football)

Translation. She worked hard and reached the goal for the
    team.
Metaphor. He got a hole-in-one. (golf).
    Translation. He succeeded on the first attempt, despite requiring
    an average of four attempts by most people.

Conferences offer unparalleled networking opportunities for attendees.
(© Monkey Business Images | Dreamstime.com)

14

Networking at the Conference

Networking may be more important than publishing.

Introduction

Presenting papers and listening to papers being presented are things to do at conferences. So, what else do people do at a conference? The answer is different for different people. In addition to attending the presentations of fascinating topics, there are often opportunities to view the exhibits area, attend tutorials, experience some of the conference's social activities, visit relatives in the city, and, most importantly, *network*. Conferences have many more publishing dimensions than traditional journal and book publishing, due to the quick turnaround, oral presentation, immediate feedback, and the opportunity for networking. At conferences, you can meet the experts in your discipline, the professors you may want to study under, the authors who wrote key books in your field, other graduate students who are having difficulty with their dissertations, the hiring managers that you might eventually want to work for, or people you might want to hire. Where else could you have access to all these people in an informal format? Conferences are indeed the ideal networking opportunity. The authors strongly recommend that you bring your business cards and meet people because a major secondary activity at a conference is networking.

Background

Again, *what else* one does at a conference is different for different people. Certain individuals may be more social or more reclusive, and others may have relatives in that city that they want to visit. The authors don't recommend that you read a novel or catch up on sleep in your room but *do* strongly recommend that you bring your business cards and meet people. If you get asked to be a session chair, your first reaction should be to say *yes,* and the second should be to read Chapter 15. There are two major *what else* things to do at a conference: networking and non-conference activities. We will talk a lot about the first activity and very little about the second.

Network, Network, Network

Networking can be done in a variety of venues and there are many reasons why you would want to be networking at conferences. The many reasons will be discussed first.

Networking for Job Opportunities

The challenging economy makes it even more important to network, and networking at conferences is an ideal opportunity to meet potential employers. Some conferences do not allow postings of job openings, while other conferences have a career center as part of the meeting venue. Many have a corkboard or table for messages and allow job openings to be posted on the board or placed on the table. The authors have often seen, at smaller specialized conferences, a single-page job posting with a pile of business cards on a table near the registration booth. If the shoe fits, call the cell phone number on the business card.

This is your opportunity to talk with potential employers officially through the career center, semi-formally by arranging to meet potential employers at the conference, or informally by networking and finding out who might be interested in your expertise. Hand over your business card when you meet potential employers. They will remember you and often will hand you one of theirs. Keep it. You never know when you will need it. Later, make notes on the back about what you discussed or what you promised to send.

VIGNETTE

Early Career Contacts

Leo Mallette, EdD

Early in Leo's career, he met a manager from another company at a conference. Steve was a manager in a state where Leo thought he might want to relocate, and they exchanged business cards. Leo's relocation never materialized, but several years later, Leo and Steve found themselves working for the same company. Leo still had Steve's card and reintroduced himself, showing that he still had Steve's old card. Steve remembered Leo, and they had a special bond when working together over the years. ■

So, it is important to bring business cards to a conference. Depending on your stage in life, work, or schooling, you may not be ready for a job change and may still be struggling in developing a thesis or dissertation topic. This is one of the advantages of conferences: free dissertation advice.

Networking for Dissertation Assistance

Everyone at a conference loves a graduate student. This may be because (1) they remember the help they received from a mentor at a conference, (2) they remember how hard it was for them, and they would have liked a word of advice, (3) they are not yet to your level and aspire to reach the scholarly goal you are trying to achieve, (4) they regret stopping at the bachelor's or master's level and not trying to pursue an advance degree, or (5) they tried and failed, and they want you to do well—they don't want you to end up like they did.

This is also your opportunity to meet other graduate students in your field of expertise or others that are in a similar field and can commiserate with the pain you are experiencing. One of the larger conferences sponsored by American Educational Research Association (AERA) has a very active graduate student council that hosts a separate room at their annual conference where graduate students have a few introductory sessions, gives them a place to land between sessions, and, most importantly, for students, provides snacks!

No one is doing the same research as you are, but you will meet people who have the same interests, or have solved a similar process problem. One student shared a problem with studying in the evenings while her kids were still awake and demanding her attention. She resolved the distraction problem by doing family things until the kids were in bed and then would work on her dissertation while the kids were asleep, the TV was off, and the dishwasher was running. One night every week or three, she could devote an entire evening when she would *allow* her kids to visit Grandma. This may have allowed her less time with her children, but it was uninterrupted quality time to work on her dissertation...and Grandma loved it.

You will be a graduate student for only a small portion of your life. This is the time to meet others and commiserate about the pain you are experiencing and congratulate each other on the progress you're making. These student comrades are the ones that will be publishing papers in the next decades. Hand them a business card. They may become paper reviewers for journals and they may be the ones reviewing your journal submissions. They can also be potential co-authors.

Networking for Future Publishing Opportunities

If you presented a paper, your presentation was put into that particular session because it meshed nicely with the other presentations under a common theme. You can gain synergy in your paper by carefully listening to earlier presenters and building on their thoughts. You can also approach the other authors, hand them a business card, and suggest a joint paper for the next conference or for a peer-reviewed journal article. Meeting potential co-authors at conferences may not always be convenient. You may not want to pursue a line of research or add to your current workload, but it's always good to keep your mind open to future publishing opportunities.

Networking to Create Alliances and Partnerships

This is also the time to look for business opportunities. You will be exposed to a myriad of ideas and concepts by people who are at the forefront of your industry. Now, you may be able to create alliances or begin partnerships where you will be a principal in a new endeavor—whether that is starting a new school in Nicaragua, a new software startup company, or a new book.

In the preceding sections, the authors have discussed reasons to network at a conference. Protocol for most other parts of conferences is to listen to the presenters and learn from the material they are presenting. But in addition to doing so, also take the time to participate in the social events at a conference and talk to people at every opportunity you get. And give them one of your business cards. At this point, the authors have talked about what you would do when networking. But *where* would you do this networking?

Networking at the Exhibits Area

The exhibits area (if there is one set up) of a conference is a tremendous environment for learning directly from the people who supply the products on display. There is information available that could not be found on a company Web site. You will have an opportunity to look at the product, twiddle the knobs, flip through the pages of the book, meet the author or editor, evaluate the product, run a simulation, bounce it on the ground, and otherwise obtain information in ways that could never be done on the Internet or with a sales brochure.

This is also an opportunity to network and learn the names of key individuals at these companies. It may be a salesperson, but they may also be the acquisitions editor, or the chief designer, or a vice president of the company. It never hurts to have the business card of a key person in your list of people to contact when you need information or a job. Here is another vignette, about meeting people at conferences.

VIGNETTE

Booth Setup

Leo Mallette, EdD

At one conference, Leo saw one of the exhibitors (John) on the night before the conference whom he recognized through work contacts. John was going to the exhibits area to set up his company's booth. Leo tagged along, helped him set up the booth for about 45 minutes, and then they went to dinner. They enjoyed the evening, and it created a long lasting bond between the two that transcends regular impersonal business contacts. ∎

The exhibits area of a conference is informative and can be fun, but it can also be an employment treasure chest if you are looking for a new opportunity.

Networking at Social Functions

There are several opportunities for networking at social functions as part of most conferences. Many of them have something to do with eating—and everybody has to eat.

Breakfast. Many people are trying to wake up, go to breakfast, and look through the conference program to make last minute decisions about which sessions to attend in the morning. If you see someone or a small group with a conference badge or program, go and ask if you can join them. You can find out where they work and if they are presenting a paper today. Don't forget to give them a business card.

Lunch. Unofficial lunches are great times to get to know someone or about their company. Ask an author whom you are interested in meeting what they are doing for lunch. They may be free, busy, or already committed to a group lunch. They may invite you to join their group for lunch. It's best if you have scouted out a local place and have suggestions ready. In any case, it's a good opportunity to learn and pass out your business cards. This gives the authors the opportunity to share a couple of the contributed vignettes.

VIGNETTE

Beware of Little Old Men in the Audience

M. M. Tehrani, PhD, The Aerospace Corporation

While in graduate school, I was attending, along with few other physics graduate students, the Annual Meeting of the American Physical Society in Washington, D.C. Each of us had a paper to present. For most of us this was the first time to give a talk at a major conference, and the authors were all very proud of that. One day, during the lunch at the conference hotel's cafeteria, the authors were discussing the talk that one of had given in the morning about the ergodic processes in quantum statistical mechanics. Next to us, an elderly gentleman was having his lunch and listening attentively to our conversation. In the middle of our discussion, the old man turned to my friend and very gently said, "Very nice! May I ask you a question?" My friend responded with a tone implying that the subject was too difficult for the old man to understand. The old man persisted and after a few minutes a dialog started. Toward the end of our lunch the authors started introducing ourselves. He pulled his conference badge from his pocket that said: E. P. Wigner. Our jaws dropped, and it took us few embarrassing moments to realize that the authors were in the presence of Eugene Paul Wigner, a giant of 20th-century physics and one of the founders of quantum mechanics. ■

VIGNETTE

Attendees Probably Had More Knowledge than I on the Subject

Ray M. Valadez, Pepperdine University Faculty

My second and solo conference paper was no less nerve-racking or without apprehension than the first. In fact, the subject matter was one in which the audience was well versed and some attendees probably had more knowledge than I on the subject. So, this made me even more nervous than when I presented my first paper. However, I explained to the audience that this was my first presentation on the subject and acknowledged that some of them may have more insight on the subject. So, I made the presentation a collaborative effort and opened the dialog by introducing several theories with known authors' positions that I knew would satisfy most of the attendees. Once I saw their faces and body language wanting to help me, I then presented my thoughts on the matter. ■

Breaks. There are often mid-morning and mid-afternoon breaks between paper sessions. This is a good time to casually chat with several people as they are getting coffee or water. Do not interrupt people who are making a beeline to the bathroom.

Dinner. This is the same as for lunch, but you may have the time to change into more casual clothes. If you get invited to a group function, you may end up in a group with someone famous whom you might have never met otherwise. Again, it's a good opportunity to learn and to pass out your business cards. In addition to the casual meals on your own, there are also the official conference meals. The awards luncheon or dinner banquet are more formal events with speeches, a keynote speaker, or award presentations, but there is still plenty of time to talk. Again, network, network, network.

Open House (sometimes called "hospitality suite"). The authors feel that it is socially irresponsible to miss these. These are catered events that bring people together, and they are usually sponsored by one company. They can be held in a hotel suite or in one of the conference rooms. Food is usually provided, ranging from finger food to a full buffet dinner. Don't be a glutton. People will remember your manners. There is often a bar—it may be an open bar (where drinks are free) or a cash bar (where you pay for the drinks; yes, even soft drinks and water). Never drink to excess. People will remember your behavior.

VIGNETTE

Meeting the Competition

Leo Mallette, EdD

Hospitality suites are social times when you can meet people that you might not normally meet. Leo once met Marv—his counterpart from a competing, rival company. There would normally be no opportunity to meet this person and discuss their jobs. Fortunately, they found themselves at the food table in a hospitality suite, introduced themselves, and were able to discuss some of their common problems without divulging any company proprietary information. ■

The Hotel Bar. Many people arrive at the conference hotel during the day or evening before the conference begins. Glance in the bar or hotel lobby, and you might find someone you know or recognize from a previous conference. Introduce yourself, but keep a professional profile.

Special Conference Events. Conferences may sponsor tours of local companies or local attractions, visits to historic sites, or a golf tournament.

Don't underestimate the value of networking at special conference-sponsored events.

Poster Sessions. Poster sessions are intended to share information between the author and the participants in a small, sometimes one-on-one setting. This is generally a good time to network and meet people, but conversations that are not related to the topic being presented should be kept to a minimum, as the author may be needed to discuss his topic with someone else. Don't ask an author at a poster session for a job interview. Be aware of your surroundings. If you are monopolizing a poster-session author's time and you see others waiting to chat, then politely stand down. (For example, "Thanks, Diane. I see there are others waiting to talk to you. Here is my card; I'll call you next week about the statistical methods you are using.") Or ask the others to join the conversation ("Hi, we were just talking about Diane's results. What do you think about her survey on the *no child left behind* program?")

Etiquette at Meals. All of us have certain habits when we eat with our family or friends. Eating buffalo wings with fraternity friends may be different from eating Thanksgiving turkey dinner with your girlfriend and potential future in-laws. There are certain eating customs that some of us were not properly taught (or that we forgot during the unending string of semesters). There are dozens of books on etiquette and manners. You should be able to find one in your library or online. The authors do not expect you to buy an etiquette book and study it, but find the information in a book or online and learn proper behavior at meals. The intent is to be seen as a professional. Knowing that you take the napkin that is on your left and that you start with the outside fork are simple rules to learn, and doing so will make you more comfortable with people who will be your peers after you graduate. When in doubt, wait and watch what other people are doing. For example, many people will not start their meal if everyone does not have food in front of them. Consider a table set for 10 people. You might appear to have poor manners if you start eating as soon as you get your chicken and vegetables, but the whole table has not been served and the other people at your table are waiting for the entire table to be served.

In the previous sections, the authors discussed meals as a vehicle for networking, and you may be ingesting more calories than you normally do, so you may want to continue or increase (or restart) your exercise regimen. You can

> **Etiquette during Meals**
>
> When in doubt, wait and watch what other people are doing.

choose from golf, the spa, the exercise room in the hotel, swimming, a brisk walk, or jogging. Some of these are good networking opportunities, too.

The Follow-Up to Networking

Write the name of the conference (initials are fine) and the year on the front of the business cards you received, and write notes on the back of the card. Indicate that you volunteered to send them a paper or a link to a Web site, or that they were going to send you something. When you get home, read the back of all your cards and promptly complete the action(s) you promised. File the card after you have completed the action.

During the week after the conference, it is good etiquette to send a note or e-mail to individuals who made an effort to talk to you or help you, even if neither of you had any actions. Tell them how they helped you and ask for more help if you think of something you needed. If you send a real (paper and ink) note, don't forget to include your business card.

Another way to connect following a conference is to use one of the many social networking sites (SNS) available through the Internet, including LinkedIn, Facebook and Twitter, among others. You can blog and tweet to build and expand your personal world of virtual communication. If you are not yet part of social networking (SN), it's time to get connected! Approximately 60 percent of Americans are regularly interacting on an SNS, and the numbers continues to grow across all segments of the population (Core 2008). SN is here to stay.

Non-Conference Activities

The authors won't dwell on this section because there usually is not much time for non-conference activities. Usually the authors have to pack up and get back to classes, or work, or family responsibilities as soon as the last session is complete. However, the authors have found that you can do some tourist activities because conferences are held in interesting places. You can take a city tour, or arrange to visit universities, companies, family, friends, or former classmates that live in the area.

VIGNETTE

A Visit with His Favorite Uncle

Leo Mallette, EdD

At a recent conference near Washington, D.C., Leo asked his nephew Adam to drive about an hour from his home in Maryland to the conference site on a particular evening. They had not seen each other since a family reunion several years previously. They had dinner together, discussed family, their work, real estate investing, and generally renewed their friendship. ■

People may think you are having a leisurely time at a conference — after all you have only one paper to present, but you will find that you will be happy to return to work to rest up from all the traveling, finding sessions, listening, preparing, presenting, talking, eating, and networking you have been doing at the conference.

Summary

The authors have identified two broad categories of *what else* one does at a conference—networking and non-conference activities. The authors discussed the first activity in more detail and discussed the second in very little detail. The authors don't recommend that you catch up on reading or sleep in your room, but *do* strongly recommend that you bring your business cards and meet people. In addition to attending the presentations of fascinating topics, there are generally opportunities to network for job opportunities, for dissertation assistance, for future publishing opportunities, and to create alliances and partnerships. Networking can be done in the exhibits area and at any of the many social functions at conferences. Experience some of the conference's social activities, and be sure to follow up your networking by fulfilling promises you made and sending thank you e-mails or notes. And *don't forget your business cards!*

Bibliography

Core LLC. "Core Finds that Americans Expect Companies to Have a Presence in Social Media," http://www.coneinc.com/content1182, (cited August 24, 2009).

Timekeeping is an important responsibility during presentations at conferences. (© Felix Mizioznikov | Dreamstime.com)

15

How to Be the Best Session Chair

If you get asked to be a session chair, your only reaction should be to say "Yes!"

Introduction

The function of a session chair is to lead the session—you will introduce the session and the presenters, keep the session moving according to a pre-arranged schedule, and you must do this in a courteous and professional manner. This chapter will help you to be the best session chairperson. Use these guidelines, but bear in mind that each conference is different and that it may be useful to observe how other session chairs do it too. This chapter discusses the tasks you do and problems you may encounter.

Audiovisual Preparation

There are very few things that are more annoying to the presenter and the audience than audiovisual (AV) equipment that doesn't work or that the presenter doesn't know how to use. Make sure you get there early, learn how to use the AV equipment, have the presenters load the presentations early, test the microphone, laser pointer, and try a sample presentation.

USB Drive. Most people will bring their presentations to the conference on a USB drive.

Session chair

The session chair will introduce the session and the presenters and keep the session moving according to a pre-arranged schedule in a courteous and professional manner.

Projector. Conferences will usually have a laptop computer and a projector for the presentations. They will often have a remote control for advancing the slides, and this may contain a built-in laser pointer. (The authors have found that the laser pointer is usually quite weak.)

Laser Pointer. It would be good to bring one, in case the conference does not supply one or if the light is inadequate due to overused batteries.

Microphone. Larger venues will have a wireless lapel microphone. Make sure the presenter has it at the right level (close to her mouth).

There may be other devices, such as a DVD or video player. Showing movies on a laptop is convenient, but the speakers (if not tied to a larger system) are inadequate for a large room. Below are some of the other activities you are responsible for.

Introduction

Show up early. Meet the presenters and put them at ease (they may be nervous). Have them load their presentations onto the laptop computer. Tell them how you will notify them that their presentation time is almost done. Have a copy of the conference program with you, and make sure you have pronounced all the names, out loud, *before* the session. If you have difficulty with any of the names, find the presenter and ask her how they would like her name pronounced. One of the authors of this book once had a conference presenter whose name was Sunddip. The author pronounced it *Sun-Dip* and was corrected; it was *Sun-Deep.*

Session Introduction. Stand at the front of the room at the start time. Be prompt. You may need to tap a glass, the microphone, or something similar to get everyone's attention. Then say, "Welcome to session (*name or number*) of the (*name*) conference. I am (*your name and affiliation*) and will be your session chair." You should remind people to turn off their cell phones, and you may want to add a sentence (but keep it short) about how the papers in your session tie together.

One of the rules of presenting is to never leave the podium empty. The session chair should stay at the front of the room until the presenter has arrived and is ready to present. It is nice to shake hands, but it is not necessary. Likewise, at the end, meet the departing presenter before he leaves and stay at the front until the next presenter has been introduced and is ready.

Presenter Introduction. Tell people the list of authors, their affiliation, the name of the presenter, and the title of the paper. It is best if you read the names and titles directly from the program. If there are more than three authors, then you should probably just introduce the presenter by saying:

- Paper number 12 is by John Smith and several co-authors from the University of Akron. John Smith will be presenting (*the paper title*).

Or, if the authors are from several different institutions:

- Paper number 12 is by John Smith from the University of Akron and several co-authors. John Smith will be presenting (*the paper title*).

While a presenter is struggling with loading his presentation, you may need to ad lib. If the presenter has handouts for the audience, you should take them from the presenter and distribute them yourself or with the help of others you ask to volunteer. Most people are willing to help distribute handouts—it gives them a chance to get up and stretch.

Titles. People can be sensitive about titles. The authors don't have a universal answer for this. Generally, the authors have noted that technical conferences are informal, but professional, meetings of peers—some have doctorates and some do not, and conferees generally do not distinguish between them, since they are all professionals. Presenters are often nervous, and addressing people by their first names should help them acclimate.

However, there are many people who need to be properly addressed when being introduced (presidents, deans, judges, members of parliament or congress, ambassadors, etc.). You probably will not be put into the position of introducing these people if you don't know the proper etiquette. Generally, a session chair will be safe if she reads the presenter's name and title exactly as written in the program.

Time Management

This is the most important function of a session chair. The session has a known number of papers for presentation and a finite number of minutes before the next session, break, or lunch. The time should be evenly divided between the presenters, allowing enough time for questions and answers. For example, if you have three presenters in a one-hour session, then you might break it up as follows:

- 1 minute to load computer with presentation, for people to take their seats, and for you to introduce the session
- 57 minutes for presentations: 19 minutes per presenter
- 2 minutes to spare

From this top-level session breakdown, you might break up the 19 minutes of each presenter's time as follows:

- 45 seconds for you to read the list of authors, their affiliations, introduce the presenter, and read the title of the paper, while the presenter comes up to the front
- 14 minutes until you give the presenter a 2-minute warning
- 2 minutes for the presenter to finish
- 15 seconds for applause and for you to ask the audience for Q&A.
- 2 minutes for Q&A and a last applause

   Make sure your presenters know the method you will use to notify them that their time is running out. The end-of-time may be indicated with either lights, timer, pointing at your watch, flash cards, waving your arms, holding up two fingers, or softly saying, "Two minutes." The authors recommend that you have an index card with the number 2 written on one

> Time management is the most important function of a session chair.

side and *Time's Up* on the other side. Do not hold this card at your chest level because the presenter will certainly not see it. Hold the card above your head and make sure the presenter has seen the card and acknowledged seeing it—this is usually a brief pause as she focuses on the card. If you don't have cards, hold up two fingers (the peace sign) above your head and softly say, "Two minutes." There is a section below on how to handle long-winded presenters (and other problems you might encounter). When the presenter has finished, start the applause and move immediately into the Q&A session.

Discussant

Discussants are rarely used, but you should know about them. A discussant is a member of the conference who has read the paper before the presentation and has listened to the presentation. The discussant's job is to professionally critique the written paper and the oral presentation immediately after the presentation is complete. This usually takes five minutes. The reviews can be benevolent or cutting. Your job as a session chair is to introduce the discussant—usually their name and affiliation are sufficient. Thank them when they are done and move immediately into the Q&A session.

Question and Answer (Q&A)

You have to decide (or you will be told) that the Q&A period will be immediately after each individual presentation or at end of session. The authors strongly recommend doing it at the end of each presentation. People lose their train of thought after listening to three or four presentations and may not remember their question.

As a session chair, you should always have one question ready for the presenter if the audience does not. Give the audience a chance to ask questions and, if there is silence, then say: *I have a question* (and then ask it).

> **Applause**
>
> The session chair will almost certainly have to take the lead to start the applause.

Your question can be simple, and it may prime the audience or break the ice for asking questions. Knowing that you may need to ask a question forces you to listen to the presenter (it is easy to become engrossed with your timer) and will make the presenter feel good—they like simple questions. If you have time before the start of the session, you may want to ask the presenter for a suggested question.

The session chair should walk to the front of the room near the end of the Q&A session, meet the presenter before they leave, start the final applause, introduce the next presenter, and stay at the front until the next presenter is ready.

Applause

The session chair is the leader of the session but will almost certainly have to take the lead to start the applause. There is no applause when the presenter is introduced, but there are three times that you should lead the applause.

End of Talk. Often the presenter will end by saying *thank you,* but at other times he may just mumble a few closing words and then stare at the audience. It is up to you to decide when the presenter has ended and start the applause. People in the audience will take the hint.

End of Q&A. When the questions stop, or the time is up for the Q&A session, it is appropriate to say *thank you* to the presenter and start a short round of applause. This should prompt him to stop taking questions, gather his material and step down.

End of Session. Once the entire program is over you should take a moment to thank everyone for coming and say: *Let's all give all the presenters another round of applause.*

You are done. You did a great job, and everyone thinks you are a seasoned session chair. The only thing left to do is add this to your résumé. However, there was one vignette submitted for this book that is very appropriate for this chapter.

VIGNETTE

Go to the Bathroom First

Victor Reinhardt, PhD

The first time I was a conference session chairman, I was a little nervous. I asked one of the old timers what was the most important things to remember as a conference session chairman. He said to me, "Go to the bathroom first. You're the only one who can't leave during the session." ■

Problem Resolution

There are many issues that can occur during a conference session, and there are no universal solutions—that's life. As the session chair, the presenters and the audience will look to you to resolve the issues. This section is written from experience and contains some suggestions for mitigating some problems that have occurred.

Long-Winded Presenter. Your primary job is to keep the session moving, and you are within your rights to interrupt a presenter if she is over her time limit. You can start with a friendly wave of a hand and a softly spoken, *"Time's up."* This can be followed by standing and a not-so-softly spoken, *"Time's up."* Then you should move to the side or center of the presenter's presentation and suggest she complete the discussion later by saying, "Unfortunately, we have run out of time, and we must conclude so the next presenter can begin. We have enjoyed your presentation, and questions can be addressed following the end of the entire session or outside the conference room." Once you have done these things and the presenter still continues to talk, there is no easy solution. Let the presenter drone on; the audience will know you did everything you could to keep the session on time. Do not touch the presenter. Stand aside, start the applause when the presenter is done, do not allow Q&A, and move immediately to the next presentation. Keep it professional.

No Show. Presenters should be there at the beginning of the session. Sometimes they are not. When it is time for their presentation, stand at the front and ask if they have arrived. If they have, then you can proceed as normal. If they have not arrived, there are two paths you can take.

1. If your conference has parallel sessions, you are expected to stay on schedule since attendees may be going from one session to another. You can continue the Q&A from the previous paper(s), or you may have to call an intermission until it is time for the next presenter.

2. If your conference does not have parallel sessions, then it is best to continue to the next presenter. This will give you more time for Q&A or allow the session to end early.

Audiovisual Problems. These can be very frustrating. The authors' recommendations are (1) to try to be somewhat familiar with the equipment, laptop, microphone, and the software (like how to go into slide show mode), and (2) know where to go for help.

Cell Phones. You respectfully informed attendees to turn off their cell phones at the beginning of the session. Most people will put it on vibrate and will still take calls during your session, but they usually step out. If they do not, it is your responsibility to go to them and ask them to step out (tap them on the shoulder and point to the door). You can open and quietly close the door for them.

Multiple Presenters. This is not a real problem unless the co-presenters both think that they have 75 percent of the time. Introduce both of the presenters and watch their time. You may want to whisper, "You have seven minutes left" when the second presenter steps up to talk.

Bad Presenter. Other than AV issues, this is probably your worst fear. A recent presenter had three issues: (1) The presenter sat behind the laptop and read her notes. As an isolated incident, this may not be a problem. If it is a problem, you can ask the presenter to stand. (2) The presenter was soft-spoken. You can ask him to speak louder, move the microphone closer to his mouth, or if there is no microphone, ask him to step closer or even into the audience. (3) The presenter was difficult to understand, and English may not have been her first language. Be respectful and professional; the presenter is doing a better job in English than you might do in her language. Give presenters support and provide encouragement.

Nervous Presenter. You can do a few things to help a nervous presenter before the session by meeting with him and addressing him by their his name. (This doesn't work with everyone.) During the session, you can make eye contact, smile, and nod your head in agreement with what he is saying—offering visual encouragement to the presenter. You may also consider pouring a glass of water and bringing it to him unobtrusively.

If the presenter loses concentration, you may have to suggest where she left off. You may have to say something such as, "You were saying that leaders are not always power hungry?" and let the presenter move back into the flow of her presentation.

Bad Graphics. This can lose an audience, and there is not much that can be done in real-time. You may want to ask the presenter to make the graphic larger, or you may want to ask, "What idea does the author want to express with this graphic?" or "Could you explain what the audience should be learning from this large table?"

Dead Time. While a presenter is struggling with loading his presentation, you may need to ad lib. Talk about the subject of the paper, why the subject is important to the audience, how it ties in to the other papers in the session, say something about the presenter, or have everyone in the room introduce themselves, if it is a very small group.

Noise from Audience. Short side discussions are normal, but conversations should not be tolerated. Get up, go to the conversationalists, and ask them (politely) to continue their conversation outside the room. They will usually terminate the conversation and listen to the presenter.

Rude Audience. Look back at the audience. Stare, shush, do a cutting motion across your throat, or in extreme situations, stand up, interrupt the presenter, and address the audience. You might say something like, "Many of us are here to hear these results. If you are not interested, could you please step outside." The authors don't ever expect this to happen.

Noise from Outside the Room. Conferences are often held in hotels, and employee access-ways are adjacent to the conference rooms. (That's how all the chairs, tables, and food get moved in and out.) They often need to move things in to set up for lunch in another room. The noise should be temporary. You may want to step in and mention they are being disruptive, if it is excessively long. If the noise is coming from the hallway, you may want to step out and see if the noise can be mitigated.

Non-Uniform Presentation Times. Some of the papers may have more background or more research to present and may have been allocated more time. Usually, you will be told about this ahead of time.

These are some of the issues that might arise when you are a session chair. Relax. Most sessions go very smoothly, and you will have no problems. This section can help you anticipate issues and how to react if you do have some problems.

Speakers' Breakfast. Many conferences have an orientation breakfast prior to the daily sessions. This is a good time to meet the presenters in your session. You should be there early, meet your presenters, help them feel comfortable, and discuss your style for notifying them that time is up.

Long-Winded Presenter—Escalation

Friendly wave of your arms and a softly spoken, "Time's up."
Stand with a louder verbal message.
Move to the side of his presentation.
Move into center, thank the presenter, suggest they complete later, or "It is time to conclude."
Stand aside, let the presenter drone on; you did everything you could to keep the session on time.
Start the applause when the presenter is done, do not allow Q&A, thank the presenter, and move immediately to the next presentation.
Keep it professional at all times!

Summary

Arrive early, start the session on time, introduce the presenters, watch the time to keep presenters on schedule, applaud at the right times, and handle the question and answer sessions. Then go home and update your résumé.

You are a published author. It's time to update your resume and start on your next article. (iStockphoto.com)

16

Reflections

This book was written to introduce you to conferences and specifically to help you become a published author at a conference. Your goal should be to get articles published in top-quality, peer-reviewed journals, and a first step is to write, present, and publish a conference article. There are many steps involved, and these chapters have helped you find the conference, understand the costs and timelines, prepare an abstract and the paper, get ready for your presentation, go to the conference, present your research, and network. The presentation may seem daunting, but remember that the audience wants you to succeed. Conferences offer many opportunities that are not available in other publishing venues. These include a quick turnaround (compared to journal publication), an oral presentation to your peers, immediate feedback, and the opportunity for networking with people who you might never meet otherwise. Take your first step into the publishing landscape. You won't regret it!

Glossary

AERA. An acronym for American Educational Research Association. A 25,000 member organization for educational researchers that is concerned with improving the educational process.

APA. An acronym for American Psychological Association. In this book, APA usually refers to a style manual for professional writing. The 6th edition of the *Publication Manual of the American Psychological Association* was published in 2009. There are many other publishing styles, and you should check with the guidelines for submission for your journal or conference.

blind review. A blind review is a method used to eliminate positive or negative personal bias toward an author or institution when evaluating a paper. All references to the author(s) and their institution(s) are deleted from the abstract or paper before review. A blind review allows the paper to be evaluated solely on its own merits and not be influenced by personal or personnel biases.

call (the call). See call for papers.

call for papers (call for proposals). A printed page or Web site that describes the conference and the requirements for submitting an abstract. The call for papers usually includes the name of the conference, the location, the dates of the conference, the due date of the abstract, and submittal instructions.

company proprietary. Trade secrets, processes, formulas, software programs, drawings, schematics, failure analyses, and other proprietary information—almost anything a company does because it could be used by another company without the effort (i.e., expense) that your company put into developing that widget or service.

conference. A formal, pre-announced gathering of people sharing a common interest. For the purposes of this book, a conference also includes presentations and a published digest (proceedings) of the presented papers.

copyright. A property right that restricts others from using work created by the copyright owner—the creator of the work or his assignees.

discussant. A specific member of the audience who has read your paper beforehand and is prepared to comment on the paper and presentation after the presentation.

due date (abstract). The date that the abstract is to be submitted to the program chair. The date is usually three to nine months before the conference.

due date (paper). The date the final paper is to be submitted to the program chair. The date is usually from six months before the conference to three weeks after the conference.

IEEE. An acronym for Institute of Electrical and Electronics Engineers. A 100,000-plus member nonprofit organization of this branch of engineering.

ITAR. An acronym for International Traffic in Arms Regulations. ITAR restrictions were implemented under Section 38 of the Arms Export Control Act to control the export of defense articles and defense services. Export includes publishing.

IRB. Institutional Review Board. A university's internal review board to prevent physical or mental damage to research participants.

journal. Papers are often published in a bound format after being peer-reviewed by two or more experts in the field and modified (per the review comments).

opportunity cost. The authors attempt to define opportunity cost by asking the question, "What else could I be doing with the time I spend preparing and going to the conference?"

parallel session. These occur when papers are being presented in separate rooms at the same (parallel) time.

peer reviewed. An independent review of the article before publication by non-author by people who are experts on the subject of the article.

primary publication. Document that is peer reviewed, first-time published, broadly disseminated, retrievable, methods explained, and can be duplicated.

publishing landscape. The environment in which you can publish. The publishing landscape includes conferences, journals, books (fiction, nonfiction, romance, travel, cooking, children's, etc.), magazines, book reviews, newspapers, letters to the editor, and online sites such as Web sites, blogs, diaries, and so on.

refereed. See peer reviewed.

session chair. The function of a session chair is to lead the session, which includes introducing the session and presenters and keeping the session moving according to a pre-arranged schedule in a courteous and professional manner.

significant other. The authors use the term significant other throughout this book. This term can apply to anyone who could become your conference traveling companion such as your husband, wife, lover, partner, friend, companion, roommate, coworker, child, parent, sibling, and so on.

SPELIT. An acronym for remembering the six key points of view for an environmental analysis of an organization: social, political, economic, legal, intercultural, and technological.

trade secrets. A type of proprietary information that has economic value, and which the owner has taken reasonable measures to protect.

Index

About the Authors

Leo Mallette received his EdD from Pepperdine University, has worked in the aerospace industry in the Los Angeles area for 33 years, and is an adjunct faculty at Pepperdine University. He has authored over 60 conference publications, co-authored the book *The SPELIT Power Matrix,* and authored the pictorial history book *Images of America: Rancho Mirage, California.* See his Web site at http://writingforconferences.com.

Clare Berger is finishing her doctoral dissertation in organizational leadership at Pepperdine University. Ms. Berger serves as communications director for a higher-education organization in California serving approximately 34,000 students and has over 15 years of experience in a variety of environments, including administration, operations, legal, marketing, and public relations.